Life Goes On...Thankfully

Life Goes On...Thankfully

A Biographical Memoir of Richard Heimler as Told to Bonnie Adler

Life Goes On...Thankfully
A Biographical Memoir of Richard Heimler
as Told to Bonnie Adler

Copyright © 2020 by Bonnie Adler
Bonadler5@gmail.com

All rights reserved. This book or any portion thereof may not be reproduced or used in any manner whatsoever without the express written permission of the publisher except for the use of brief quotations in a book review.

This biographical memoir reflects Richard Heimler's recollections of his experiences over time, as recorded in the last eighteen months of his life by the author, Bonnie Adler. Although it was Richard's intent to present the whole truth and nothing but the truth, human memory is faulty. Richard acknowledged that well-meaning people can honestly disagree about words spoken or the details of events. The dialogue in this book is not presented as a word-for-word transcript of conversations, but in all cases, it evokes the meaning and feeling of conversations as Richard recalled them.

Cover design by Miggs Burroughs

Printed in the United States of America

First Printing, 2020

ISBN 9781658167475

To Richard Heimler, whose passion for "making memories" left us all richer. No one who knew him will ever forget him.

Introduction: Curtain Up

I was poking around a giant summer sale in Stamford, Connecticut, when I heard someone call my name. I looked up and felt a shock of recognition paired with an electric burst of delight. "Richard! How wonderful to see you again." I did a quick calculation. "It's been at least fifteen years."

Without missing a beat, he laughed and said in his familiar, friendly way, "You'd never know it from the way you look. You haven't changed at all. You look fantastic!"

We hugged, and I felt overjoyed to see him, just as I always did all those years ago when we were good friends living in the same suburban town in New Jersey. I appraised him surreptitiously. I knew he had been sick. He looked well, though; tall, dark, good-looking, and very happy. He was with his mother, Audrey, whom I also remembered as a frequent visitor to his home. She immediately asked about my daughter, who was the best friend of Richard's little girl, Rachel. His wife, Jodi, had been my closest friend in those years when we were both dizzy with the demands of small children. We, too, had lost touch.

After paying me some more outsized compliments and tossing off a few jokes, leaving me flattered and a bit dazzled, Richard said, "I live right there." He pointed to an elegant high-rise nearby, "with my husband, Chris. You'll have to meet him."

"I'd love that," I said, thinking of my old friend, Jodi.

We promised to get together, and we actually did, this time at my home in nearby Westport. Chris, Richard's new husband, was as attractive as Richard and equally delightful. They gave off an air of radiance and glamour, and we talked and laughed with ease. Richard was proud to show me his new wedding ring, which was identical to the one Chris wore. "It's strange to tell someone I have a husband," he said. "I'm still getting used to it."

Of course, I asked about Jodi and learned she had a boyfriend but had not remarried. His son, Michael, a year younger than my son, was engaged to be married in a few months.

I confess I had an ulterior motive when I arranged our get-together. I was writing a book about secrets, and I hoped Richard would allow me to include his in my book. When I asked him, he replied easily that he would be happy to share the story of his coming out with me. *I never say no when I can say yes*, were his exact words. *Especially if I can help other people.*

I was drawn to the subject of secrets. I had always pondered the stifling confusion wrought by silence or worse, outright deception. When I was a child, my parents had denied me the stories of their lives in Hitler's concentration camps, in fear of hurting me.

Later, my son carried his own secret for years, afraid to tell us he was gay. He observed with silent anxiety the not-so-few closeted fathers he met in our town who lived life as straight, married men, and he was determined not to live his own life trapped in a lie. One day, he summoned the courage and asked if his father and I would still love him regardless of his sexual orientation.

Our son was luckier than Richard Heimler was. Times had changed in the single generation from Richard's to his.

The interviews with Richard began. The first thing Richard presented me with was a Myers-Briggs Personality Assessment he had taken, which identified him as an extrovert. I laughed. That was an understatement, as I recalled, but I could tell he was excited about our plan to document his story.

As early as our first meeting, however, I understood there were two stories, not one. The first was the story of the charming husband and father, pillar of the Jewish community, who dared to ask for recognition and acceptance as he overturned his life to live openly as a gay man.

The other, perhaps even larger tale was his subsequent diagnosis of serious illness, and his determination to be a leader in the fight against cancer despite the stigma he felt and the real threat of death. Both stories reflected an extraordinarily brave, determined person who wanted to make a difference in the world as he knew it. I immediately made up my mind to give up my original plan and to write his story in its entirety. He was committed to the plan as well.

It took courage for Richard to tell me about the agony behind his decision to come out and even more to share his battle with illness. Once, after a sudden serious setback, he left a message on my voice mail. He said, "Hi Bonnie...It's Richard. As you can see, I'm not dead yet. I'm calling to tell you we can go on with the book." And thus, I became the keeper of his story.

It took commitment for me to record his words and create a cohesive narrative that would honor this remarkable life. Often, during our weekly discussions, I could not hold back my tears. Other times I wanted to run, as I understood the angst and pain he faced in fighting his illness.

Mostly, we met in his apartment in Stamford, sitting at his dining room table near a window that offered a sweeping view of the city. Sometimes we conducted our interviews via Skype, continuing on whether it was he or I who was traveling. Often, when our regular two-hour interviews ended, I needed to sit alone in my car or in a coffee shop to absorb his words, the gravity of his situation, and the bravery with which he faced it.

I was afraid of so much truthfulness and moved by the strength it took for him to speak with as much honesty as he could muster. I was concerned that I would "out" him, hurt him by telling the unvarnished details of his life. But I also knew Richard's story had become important not just to him, but to his family, who urged him to continue his quest to share his tale with the world. And so I resolved to continue, no matter how difficult it might be.

Perhaps he did not realize at first how much he would come to care about our interviews. I believe it was serious illness that made him more resolute than ever to leave his mark in this world. He wanted to proclaim himself a gay man and a cancer survivor, one unashamed of either definition in a world afraid of both. He was determined to make his life with either label a proud one.

I confess that like so many others, I was probably a little bit in love with him. And why not? He was so dashing, and he possessed a quick and wicked sense of humor. He was irreverent, occasionally naughty, and always brave. His story was compelling, too. He lived with a secret—until he did not, and then he had to fight to survive.

The following pages are Richard's story as he told it to me, an intoxicating tale of laughter, love, sex, money, danger, and ultimately, of strength and human dignity. I am honored to have collaborated with him to tell it.

—Bonnie Adler

One

The Best Little Boy in the World

"Richard! Richard!"

I could hear my mother calling me and growing increasingly frantic. Then she came upon me and laughed. I was right where she had left me, of course, in our back yard, moving myself gently back and forth in our toddler swing, kicking my feet, looking up at the trees above, and talking to myself.

"I forgot all about you, Richard," she said. "I was busy watching your brothers. And here you are, just fine, smiling up at the sky."

I looked at her with joy and held my arms out to her. "Mamma!"

It was a rare moment of peace, rare enough to remember years later. Mostly, I was the runt of the litter at home, surrounded by two boisterous older brothers and then, five years later, another, younger one, who grew up idolizing and imitating them, not me. We were named Ronald, Randy, Richard, and Robert, which my mother thought was a clever idea, but in fact made it impossible for most people to tell us apart, let alone call us by the correct name.

We grew up in the 1960s, in Hewlett, New York, a wealthy suburb on Long Island. Hewlett was one of the Five Towns, an exclusive cluster of villages close to Manhattan known for high real estate values, good schools, and spoiled Jewish kids. But the relative wealth we may have enjoyed compared with others growing up in New York did not come without responsibilities.

We Heimler boys were raised with a strict moral code and the clear understanding that the privilege in our lives was not to be taken for granted. First of all, we were required to be decent and considerate human beings, to present ourselves as clean and neat, with good manners and the ability to look people in the eye when we were spoken to. We also had to take school seriously, do our homework, be kind to others, and respect our elders.

In addition, we had to be good Jewish boys, which meant Hebrew school several times a week after public school and, at the age of thirteen, having a Bar Mitzvah. We had to learn that not everyone had luck, money, youth, good health, and love in their lives, and we were expected to pitch in if we could be of any help to others.

It was a long list of requirements, but the most fundamental was the implicit command that we not deviate from a certain, predictable path. We were to grow up without getting into trouble, go to college, find a lucrative career, marry a good Jewish girl, have children, and give back when possible to the world around us.

And I bought into it all, hook, line, and sinker. I wanted my parents, especially my mother, whom I adored, to be proud of me. I wanted to be the best little boy in the world. I believed fervently in happy endings. This made me a placid child, a misfit among my unruly brothers, who loved crashing around and creating havoc. Because of that, I rarely got into trouble, despite my parents being strict. It just was not my nature. From my earliest days, I just wanted to make everyone happy.

~

Before I was even ten years old, I discovered that I was attracted to males. I knew this from my interest in my father's *Penthouse* magazines, which I found in the back of a drawer in my parents' bathroom. I flipped through the pages, knowing that I was snooping and had found something illicit. However, I soon realized that what was illicit was my rapt interest in the pictures of the men and their erect, engorged penises, not the pictures of the big-breasted and voluptuous women. I knew with certainty to keep this interest to myself, and to make no mention of it to my brothers or my father.

I never felt close with my father, who seemed more interested in my brothers and their sports activities than in me. He was also preoccupied with the family business, a costume-jewelry manufacturing company started by his father, which was growing into a very lucrative business.

My love for my mother came as naturally to me as my own breath. She was dark haired, small, slender, and fine featured. She was a beautiful woman and very strong-willed and confident. She was often called on to protect me from my brothers, which she did fiercely and without hesitation. She was like a lioness who protected me. Once she came home just as my brothers were about to try something they thought would be funny.

"Hey, Richard, come here," said Randy. "We've got some great candy for you."

Ronnie had a string in one hand and a Milky Way chocolate bar in the other.

"We're going to tie this string around your teeth and pull you up the second-floor staircase by the string. If you get your feet off the ground, we'll give you this Milky Way."

Just as I was doubtfully considering this proposition, my mother came into the hallway. Her eyes narrowed, and her small frame seemed to swell as she assessed the situation. She did not ask for an explanation. She knew instantly who was guilty and levied the punishment with 100 percent accuracy on Ronnie, the eldest.

"Are you out of your mind? Do you want to break his neck?"

They both shrank back, splashed by the icy hose of her anger. I was left with the disquieting feeling of gratitude that she had rescued me but sadness, too, because once again, I was the odd man out with my brothers.

She was my great defender, and I always felt safe in her presence. She was meticulous, thorough, and very well organized. She kept us all in clean clothing, good health, and on a firm schedule. She always looked her best, and she loved to wear beautiful clothing. My mother was a renegade for her time, though. She wanted to work, unlike so many of the moms in our neighborhood.

Once I overheard a conversation she had with my father about a bill he got from Bonwit Teller.

"Audrey," he said, shaking his head. "What is this? What did you buy?"

She stiffened up and became silent just long enough for him to know she resented his question. "You know that dress I wore to the club Saturday night that you liked so much? That was what I bought."

It was scenes like that one that led her to decide she wanted her own income. She became an interior decorator. The furniture in our house was selected by my mother with great care. It became her first showroom. We had to be extra neat when a potential client would come to see what she had done with our house, which was why my brothers were always in the street, riding bikes and playing ball in the cul-de-sac. My mother grew her business from inception, and she made a good income, which she was very proud of.

I loved Thursdays because that was the day she went to New York to the decorator showrooms to source products and to meet clients. My grandmother came to our house every Thursday to keep an eye on us while she was out.

For as long as I can remember, I was deeply attached to my grandmother Adeline, my mother's mother. Her warmth and love felt like it was directed right at me, not at my brothers. When I was just two or three years old, I followed her around the house, and if she left me even for a moment to go to the bathroom, I waited patiently near the door for her to come out. When she did, I clapped my hands, happy to be right there again in the sight of her.

My grandmother and grandfather lived in the Midwood section of Brooklyn, a well-tended middle-class neighborhood with tree-lined side streets and small apartment buildings side by side with one- and two-family homes. They had a single-family house with a tiny kitchen, where they raised my mother and her two brothers. It was a world away from the upper-crust greenery and matching homes in the suburbs of Long Island and the chaos and frenetic activity of my own residence.

Sleepovers at my grandparents' home were my favorite, even when I was as little as three or four years old. I spent the day with my grandmother, helping her with her cooking or shopping or cleaning, always feeling as if I truly was a great help to her. She would always look at the kitchen clock in the late afternoon, paying attention to the time so she'd be ready for my grandfather's return home. Just before he was due to arrive, she would take a few moments to put on some lipstick and brush her hair.

"Richard, I just want to freshen up so that when Grandpa comes home, I don't look a fright."

"But why, Grandma? You look so pretty just the way you are!" Her hair was always short and neat, and her movements, lively and fluid. She was a grandma, but to me, her age was part of her beauty.

When my grandfather came home, she dropped everything and rushed to greet him at the front door.

"Adeline!" he'd shout and hug her tightly. He was always overjoyed to see her, no matter if he had been traveling for days or had only been gone since morning. When I witnessed this outward display of affection, I felt ecstatic, knowing that this kind of love was possible between two people. It was so expansive that it just spilled over to me.

~

My grandparents were great card players. They taught me to play gin rummy. The three of us spent endless hours playing cards at the kitchen table, our own complete circle of joy. If I was hungry, my grandmother would make me oatmeal with a bit of warm milk, which she spooned out onto a flat plate, making a happy face out of raisins.

One day, my grandmother and I were in the kitchen when my grandfather came in. "Adeline, can you make me a cup of tea?"

"Of course." She jumped up and filled the old silver teakettle with water. She ignited the pilot light, placed the kettle on the stove, and then rooted around for the tea bags, sugar, and lemon to make it just the way he liked it. As she pulled a cup and saucer from the cabinet, she spied a small blue box next to the dishes that most certainly did not belong there. She pulled it out with a shriek of joy and surprise and opened it.

Inside was a jeweled brooch, a glittering circle of diamonds, from Tiffany & Co. She swooned and jumped and hugged him. She wanted to change from her everyday house dress so she could try it on with something more elegant, but he couldn't wait. He helped her pin it on, and they laughed, because the brooch was so fancy against her plain duster.

She twirled and preened, and he grabbed her and hugged her, kissing her on the mouth right in front of me. Apparently, he'd had some good fortune at work, and his first thought was to buy something extraordinary for her.

One day, my grandmother could not find her Tiffany pin. She and I turned the house upside down looking for it, sure that if we looked hard enough, we'd find it. But it was nowhere to be found. My grandfather never said it had been expensive or that she was careless. Instead, he bought her another one, exactly the same as the one she had lost.

A few years later, during the days-long preparation for the Passover holiday, which required cleaning the entire kitchen literally from floor to ceiling, my grandmother climbed up on a stool to clean the shelves that were normally out of reach. And there was the Tiffany pin, sitting inside a gravy boat, where she had put it so many moons ago. She had been wearing it one day when she began some impromptu housework and didn't want it to get dusty. She had forgotten the entire episode. When my grandfather heard the news of its recovery, he couldn't have cared less that she had two identical pins. She could do no wrong in his mind.

Sometimes he took my grandmother along with him on business trips, so she could keep him company. Once they were gone for eight weeks, just the two of them, alone together on the road. They never tired of each other, never ran out of things to say or moments to share. It was a love I always hoped to be able to recreate in my own life.

They often came to visit us at home in Hewlett.

When I was really little and it was time for my grandparents to go home, I cried because I wanted to go back to their house with them. If they came on a weekend, sometimes they pretended to kidnap me.

"Shhh...Richard. Be very quiet," said my grandmother, as she put me in my pajamas.

She wrapped me in a blanket and carried me down to the car, where my grandfather was waiting, with the engine of his big Chevrolet running.

"Stay very still," she whispered, and she deposited me in the passenger seat right up front next to my grandfather. "Hide!"

Eyes shut tight, I shrank down, disappearing below the window so no one could see me. My grandmother climbed into the back seat.

"Let's drive around the block to make sure the police aren't looking for you."

Eventually, while my heart was pounding so I could hardly breathe, they declared the all clear.

"Okay, Richard. It's safe now. You can get in the back seat."

They stopped the car and moved me to the back seat. My grandmother got in front, next to my grandfather, and we would escape to Brooklyn.

The next day, Sunday, they devoted exclusively to me. Often, they gave me a torturous choice: go to the nearby toy store on Avenue J or go to the arcade in Coney Island to play Skee-Ball. Toy store? What treasures would they get me? I loved all the whistles, kazoos, crayons, coloring books, and puzzles, and they always bought me whatever I asked for.

Or should I pick Coney Island, the great rides, and Skee-Ball? My grandmother had a special trick—a skillful flick of the wrist that inevitably got the heavy Skee-Ball up the slender, black rubber incline, into the winning fifty-point hole, and ultimately, generating a big game score that earned little coupons that could be exchanged for treasures such as stuffed animals, baseball hats, whistles, or any manner of prizes.

At Christmastime, the factories in New York would slow down or close, and my parents would take us on exciting trips. We frequently went to Florida and Puerto Rico. One Christmas, when I was in kindergarten, our family took a split vacation. My grandparents took my brother Randy and me to Puerto Rico while my parents took my two other brothers to Florida.

My mother packed all our best clothing, and we even had a camera for the trip to San Juan. All went well until the trip home. On the way back to Kennedy Airport—Idlewild, in those days—there was a sudden booming explosion on the plane. The flight attendants immediately instructed the passengers to prepare for a crash landing, and panic ensued. People were screaming while the flight attendants got ready to orchestrate an emergency escape into life rafts floating in the frigid water below. Women and children were instructed to exit first, through the rear of the plane.

A passenger in the row ahead of us had been drinking heavily during the flight. As we got ready to move to the back of the plane, he stood up and lunged at me and my brother, trying to get ahead of us and closer to the emergency exit.

Life Goes On...Thankfully

My grandmother reached back and punched him right in the face. "Don't you dare touch those kids!"

Apparently cowed, he listened to her. I had never even heard her raise her voice before.

Our plane landed with its nose in the frigid waters of Jamaica Bay, off Brooklyn and Queens, New York. A very large inflatable life raft had been activated and was waiting for us in the water. My grandfather, who had disappeared from my sight during the melee, had volunteered to catch passengers as they jumped from the plane onto an inflated slide and slid into our rickety lifeboat. When we were at the emergency exit, we saw him below.

He called out to us. "Everything will be okay. I'm right here. Just slide down the ramp as if you were on a sliding pond in the park. I'll catch you; I promise." With that, the three of us slid into his waiting embrace.

We got home at 4:00 a.m., the latest I had ever been up. My mother, glad we were safe, nevertheless regretted that we never got our luggage back, especially since she had packed our best and newest clothes.

In an odd combination of crisis and resolution, she insisted that I go to school the very next day.

"Mom," I said, when she woke me up. "I'm tired. I was up till four o'clock in the morning. And I was in a plane crash! I was floating in the water! Can't I stay home from school?"

"No. You're fine. Get up and get moving. Besides, you'll be able to tell your teacher and your friends what happened."

After all, we were alive, and the daily routine was always a source of comfort and control for her.

Several days later, we mailed our vacation photos out to be developed by Kodak in Rochester, New York, which was the way things were done in the 1960s. The company sent our film back undeveloped, with a note that read, "Please take better care of your film. Despite our best efforts, wet film cannot be developed."

Two

First Broadway Show

In 1966, when I was six years old, I saw my first Broadway show, *Superman*. My grandparents took me, each holding one of my hands as we navigated the streets of then-decaying Times Square. My eyes widened at the crush of dilapidated buildings and old winos and drug addicts mixing with well-heeled theatergoers. We moved quickly past the triple-X porno shops, the three-card monte dealers, and the pickpockets. A disheveled man with ragged hair and filthy clothes came right up to us, begging for some money.

My grandfather held my hand tightly and said, "I don't have any money," and we hurried along. But I was upset.

"Grandpa," I said. "Is it true? Do you really have no money?"

He looked at me and then stopped and hugged me. "Richard," he said, "don't worry. I do have money, but I didn't want to give it to him because we were late for the show. If we see him on our way back, I'll give him some."

I sat in the darkened theater between my grandparents, holding onto my first *Playbill*. I remember a scrim, a blue set piece, like a curtain. A mini Superman flew across it. I sat in the audience, captivated by the handsome man of steel in full dress uniform, a splendid combination of power and kindness. He was so handsome, so strong, and so controlled. He was also a hero with a secret, a man with two identities, an example I would connect to later.

This was the first time I felt the magic of the theater, a feeling that stayed with me from that day forward.

There followed in my life a panoply of America's greatest musical theater. I saw them all: *The Sound of Music*; *Annie*; *Peter Pan*; *Fiddler on the Roof*; *Mary Poppins*; *Funny Girl*; *Man of La Mancha*; *Hello, Dolly*; *Pippin*; and *Mame*. Every time it was the same. The theater darkened, the curtain went up, and for the next two or three hours, I gave myself over to the story—the soaring emotion, the slow buildup of the music and the climactic numbers, and the optimism, and embrace of human concerns. I was part of something far bigger than myself every time I was there.

When the film *Hello, Dolly* was released, I was nine years old. I wanted desperately to go. I knew it was playing at the Loewe's theater, a huge art deco cinema in Brooklyn. Every day I cut out the *Hello, Dolly* movie ad from the newspaper and mailed it to my grandmother. "Take me!" I'd scrawl across the ad.

Of course, she did as I asked. One of the hit numbers in the score is called, "When the Parade Passes By." I was so overcome by the scene in the movie that I jumped up and saluted the screen as if I, too, were a spectator at the parade.

By the time I was twelve, I had seen enough Broadway shows to create a collage out of my growing collection of *Playbills* for a school project. The central element in the collage featured a play called *The Me Nobody Knows*, which I saw when I was eleven years old. The show offered a series of vignettes about misfit kids from broken homes looking for their places in life. I had begun to feel a strong connection to characters who were misunderstood, who had strong inner voices and introspective thoughts and wanted, above all, to be valued.

Of course, the title struck me as well, because I, too, had a fleeting awareness of a "me" nobody knew. I knew I had feelings that other boys didn't share, that in some deeply secret way, I was a misfit. I would repeat to myself, "I'm nearsighted, I'm right-handed, and I'm attracted to men." It was my mantra, so to speak. I did not realize the significance. I thought it was just a little part of who I was.

I saw *Pippin* in 1973 when I was thirteen. It was about a prince who longed for greatness but had no idea how to achieve this goal. Ultimately, he realized that one cannot decide to become great, but must discover greatness within.

"My Corner of the Sky," the hit song from *Pippin*, became one of my favorites. The lyric, "I want my life to be something more than long," emblazoned itself in my adolescent soul. I did not really understand my alienation, but just like Pippin, I desperately wanted to find my corner of the sky, where my spirit could run free. I just wasn't sure how I would get there.

Three

Puberty

Occasionally I would admit to myself that I was attracted to men in a way that was not normal. It was an interest that I knew to keep to myself. My brothers certainly did not share this or any of my most passionate interests. They did not care particularly for theater, and they certainly did not lay claim to my grandmother the way I did. They were far better athletes than I and were almost exclusively focused on sports. My father went to all of their weekend games, and he would talk about them afterward with excitement and evident pleasure. While he took me to the theater occasionally, it was always with my mother, and I could feel he was doing it from a sense of obligation.

I also lived by a self-imposed guiding principle that held me to an even stricter standard: I wanted to be the perfect boy. I wanted to be someone who made others happy, who could create joy around me and please others. I felt a passion to give of myself to others, which, in turn, made me happy.

I wanted to be the best little boy in the world, and as I grew older, I clung to that concept because it brought me, as well as others, great joy. I refused to feel the burden of it, focusing only upon the positive.

But every once in a while, something would happen that gave me pause. My interest in looking at the men in my dad's *Penthouse* magazines reminded me that something was clearly different about me, but I would not dwell on it for long. I told myself this attraction to males was just a part of me. I would repeat to myself, "I'm nearsighted, I'm right-handed, and I'm attracted to men." But I kept this mantra secret and buried deep inside. It was a conscious and unconscious reality that I dealt with only rarely.

As I began my adolescence, there were moments when these buried feelings would surface.

We often took ski trips to Massachusetts. One of my closest friends, Jeff, was invited along and was my roommate on one of our family vacations. I couldn't control my excitement at having another male sharing a room with me. I watched him get undressed, knowing that my arousal was not something that most boys experienced.

"Jeff," I said, with as much studied indifference as I could muster. "It's freezing in here! They're too stingy to put up the heat in this cabin. Maybe we should sleep in the same bed for warmth?"

He looked at me with a mix of derision and amusement. "Are you crazy? I'm not getting anywhere near you in a bed; I don't care how cold it is. What do you think I am, a fag?"

And that was the end of that. I was lucky he was such a good friend because he did not take the opportunity to humiliate me, and he could have.

~

My first sexual experience with a man came in 1973, when I was thirteen.

I was in camp, away from home for the summer. My counselor approached and sat on my bed late at night when everyone else was asleep. Perhaps he had a sense of which boy would welcome his advances. He perched himself at the edge of the narrow bed and rubbed my leg.

"Does that feel good?" he asked me. "Is this okay?"

I nodded, aroused, barely able to breathe, afraid he would stop, afraid he would continue.

And he did continue, gently, then harder and with increasing persistence.

I rubbed him back. Before I knew it, he was masturbating me, and I felt good—wonderful, actually.

The next night, I waited for him, hoping he would come back. And he did.

Again, all the other kids were asleep. He came to me quietly in the night, and asked, "Are you awake? Can I sit on your bed?" He rubbed my leg again, and he moved to my penis again, and I let him rub me until I came.

We did that two nights in a row, but I felt guilty about it. I knew it was a bad thing. I knew I shouldn't be doing that. I didn't know how I was going to get away with it.

When he came to me on the third night, I said, "We have to stop. I'm going to get in trouble."

"No, you won't," he said, so crestfallen that I felt even more guilt. But I insisted we stop.

It was very confusing. It came out of nowhere, and I really enjoyed it. But I couldn't deal with it, and I put an end to it. Of course, I never told my parents about it, because I knew they would have had the counselor summarily fired, if not prosecuted.

The camp provided other sexual moments.

We had open showers. I got excited in the showers, seeing boys naked, although I kept my thoughts to myself and never acted on any of them. But it was uncomfortable because I feared that if I had an erection, someone would see it and say something about it.

~

In high school, I always did what I was expected to do. My grades were good. Studying and performing well on tests was easier for me than for many, and I busied myself on the school newspaper and in the theater program. I tried acting and singing, but I was stiff and awkward on stage. I couldn't carry a tune, and I got stage fright instantly. So I gravitated backstage, acting as a set designer, prop builder, and a reliable support staff for innumerable school productions.

I dated a girl called Mindy, who was very smart and pretty, with dark hair, brown eyes, and big breasts. The boys at school called her a Jewish goddess. She was very open sexually, and she liked me. I liked her because her father was my dentist, and I thought he was handsome and interesting. Mindy and I spent many evenings together at her house. Eventually, her parents would go upstairs, and we would watch TV in the den. She would creep closer to me on the couch, put her arms around my neck or throw a leg over mine while we watched *Laverne & Shirley*, *M*A*S*H*, or *All in the Family*.

"Richard," she whispered, her tongue practically in my ear. "You can kiss me if you like." She wanted to fool around, but...I wasn't up to it.

She reached over and put her hand on my pants, pressing on my penis. She loved the idea of getting me excited.

"Your parents are going to come downstairs," I said.

"No, they won't. They're asleep."

"How can you be sure?" I jumped up to go to the bathroom to break the tension. Her parents kept the best magazines in the bathroom, and I deliberately read a piece from *Vanity Fair* for way too long, to get my message across.

When I finally came out of the bathroom, she was hurt. "What's the matter with you? Why are you so worried about my parents? They'll never come down. I know it."

"I'm afraid of your mother," I said. "She's five two and weighs 110 pounds, but she'd insist we get married. You're too young! You got a score of 700 on your verbal SATs! You've got your whole life ahead of you..."

We broke up not long after that. Evidently she was not impressed with my concern for her future welfare.

~

Life Goes On...Thankfully

Once, I took another girl to see *A Chorus Line*. I took her to Sardi's for lunch beforehand. That was my idea of a good date. I did not have to be put on the spot romantically and could disguise my lack of sexual aggression with culture and conversation.

I had a lot of friends, more girls than boys, but I innately avoided anything romantic. There were some guys in my class that I was attracted to, but I never acted on my feelings. I simply carried with me an awareness that I was different. Like a shy child afraid of eye contact with a friendly adult, I kept my eyes fixed in another direction, hoping that if I didn't look, the scary thing would never enter my line of vision.

Early in my teens, my spine began to curve slowly and steadily. I began to experience back pain, and my posture was compromised. My shoulders and my hips were not aligned, and I walked with an awkward, lifted thrust to my gait. When I was sixteen, the doctors were unanimous in recommending that I wear a brace eighteen out of twenty-four hours a day. The brace extended from just below my chin to the bottom of my torso. I became self-conscious, in addition to being physically uncomfortable.

Soon after, my mother and I walked together down the main street of our town, a glossy shopping area filled with stores and people, many of whom we knew. I saw myself in the reflection of the shop windows, a tall, dark-haired, slender young man with glasses and a mouthful of orthodontia, who looked to me like he was trapped in his own personal cage. The brace was highly visible, and I was ashamed.

"Mom," I said, my face hot with embarrassment. "They are all looking at me." "Yes, they are," she said. She stopped walking, and she drew a breath. She looked me straight in the eye, as she often did when she laid down the law in our household. "But I'm going to tell you something you must never forget. They are all looking at you right now, but it doesn't matter. They will look at you just for this minute, and then they will go back to thinking about themselves. That is the way people are. You are important to yourself, but not to them. For them, you and your brace are just a fleeting thought."

After that, I stood a little straighter, for I trusted her and knew she was telling the truth. But, despite my many friends, I began to withdraw a bit, the brace forcing me to hide in the cocoon of its suffocating embrace.

I volunteered to help the elderly, forming friendships with senior citizens in my town, for whom I did odd jobs. I was the only student at Hewlett High School who offered his time and effort in a nursing home. I loved going there, listening to the stories that the seniors told me. There was a drama to the stories, to the fragility and sweetness of their lives, not unlike what I would encounter in the theater.

I formed one friendship in particular with an elderly gentleman whom I visited regularly, Pete. He was often confused and could not walk very well. He had lost his wife to cancer and had only one son who lived far away. His white hair was often in disarray, giving him a bit of the Albert Einstein look, but he loved to talk, and he spoke mostly about the wonderful wife he lost and his love for classical music.

He loved Leonard Bernstein, so I took my *West Side Story* album and a portable record player when I went to visit. He was so grateful, but I was happy to do it and listen to the music with him. When we played the song, "When You're a Jet" he leaned in and said in his raspy voice, "I was a member of a gang, too."

"What? What do you mean?"

"I grew up in a tenement on the Lower East Side. My mother raised my brother and me after my father died. She worked as a maid during the day and took in ironing for extra money at home. We were so poor that my brother and I would steal food from the vendors on the street to get enough to eat. A bunch of us kids would distract the peddlers with pushcarts on the Bowery with firecrackers, and when they weren't looking, we would steal potatoes off their carts and divide them up. I would bring home potatoes to my mother, and she made soup with them. She never asked me how I got the potatoes, and I never told her."

He loved the music I brought and knew the words to every song. When it was time for his dinner, I saw that he had trouble eating the food from his tray, so I began to feed him. At first I was awkward as I lifted the fork to his mouth and patted his lips clean. But then I got comfortable, and we laughed and joked while he ate. I felt I nourished him, and it made me happy.

A teenage boy caring about and feeding an old man was perceived as unusual. Somehow the local newspaper got wind of it and did a story on me. My brothers, unimpressed, made fun of the article.

"Richard, do you take him to the bathroom, too?" asked Randy. My mother scolded them. "What have you done to get an article written about you?" she chided. My father was silent on the matter, but I already knew he would have little in the way of a compliment for that sort of thing.

~

I have always believed that you should leave your mark wherever you go, and I threw myself into the academics and activities offered by Northwestern University with great abandon. I found endless opportunities there, finally coming into my own.

I got my buck teeth fixed and exchanged my glasses for contact lenses, and I finally stopped wearing the back brace. I looked and felt more handsome and was able to accept the compliments I began to get from girls as genuine. I joined Hillel, the Jewish youth organization, so I could meet Jewish students, have Shabbat dinners and celebrate Jewish holidays when I couldn't return to my home in Long Island. There I found friends that have stayed with me a lifetime.

I was always a football fan, and I found no end of kindred souls who shared my love of the game. My first roommate was Peter Van

Halley, who turned into a lifelong friend. I called him before we started school, so excited to connect.

"What albums are you bringing up?" I asked. Music was a barometer by which we all measured each other. Turned out he was passionate about rock music, bringing Cat Stevens, James Taylor, Carol King, Joe Cocker, and all of the most beloved music of our time—about a hundred albums in all.

"I see you've got a gap in your collection," I said. "I'm bringing *Funny Girl* and *The Sound of Music*, plus all my other Broadway show albums. I've probably got about thirty or forty." He laughed. He was fine with it, later joking that he should have known then that I was going to flip to the other side.

I participated in the Northwestern theater program, where I found my real niche and many lifelong friends. I did no acting but made a great commitment to being backstage, creating props, painting sets, assisting with tech, lighting, wardrobe, and sound. I was a natural—I loved the feeling of creating the right milieu for the performers onstage, the perfect set.

In the recesses of my mind was always the idea that I would meet the right girl at college and get married to her and have the life I had always dreamed of. I was not torn about my sexuality at Northwestern. There were certainly opportunities to meet gay men, especially in the theater department, where many guys did hit on me. But I did not permit myself any diversion or temptation. I did not reciprocate. I did not suffer over it. I simply refused to be tempted, refused to recognize that I could sway from my unwavering vision of the future.

I craved what I called the perfect white-picket-fence life, and I was determined to find the right woman with whom to share it. I wanted to be a husband, a father, and a person of integrity who made a difference in the world.

I dated a lot of women casually, but if a girl started getting too aggressive sexually, I ultimately broke up with her. I wasn't stupid; I knew what was going on, but I maintained a level of conscious and unconscious denial that was extraordinary.

Life Goes On...Thankfully

When I found Jodi, I found the life I always wanted. But it took me a while. We first met when we were both freshmen, eating at the school cafeteria. She sat down next to me and my roommate, whom she had met in an English class.

She was pretty, with dark-brown hair; big hazel eyes; honey-toned skin; and a lovely, full-figured body. She wore stretch pants and sweaters with shoulder pads, the uniform of college girls. She laughed easily and had a warm, engaging quality that I recognized instantly as happiness.

She was interested in the play she knew we were working on for the drama department. It was *Man of La Mancha*, and she wanted to know why I chose to work backstage instead of acting. I laughed.

"Just look at me," I said. "You can tell I'm no actor."

"I don't know," she said, flirting immediately, "you're tall, dark, and handsome, which is kinda what's required, isn't it?"

"Nice of you to notice, but I'm also stiff and nervous and never got one part in high school, so I'm the leading man in the backstage department," I said.

"Oh yeah? Where are you from?"

She was immediately impressed when she heard that I was from the Five Towns region. The reputation for Long Island Jewish boys with savvy had preceded me.

"I heard that's really cool," she said. "I'm just from Havertown, Pennsylvania. Ever hear of it?" Of course, I hadn't.

For Jodi, it was love at first sight, and I really liked her as well. We dated through *Man of La Mancha*, first-semester freshman English, and for her, the first "freshman fifteen."

But after a few months, I felt threatened by what I perceived was the commitment I believed she was ready for. I had always wanted to find a Jewish girl, get married, and have the job and family. But I was hesitant, and a part of me was frightened. Our relationship was easy and fun and undemanding.

I did not have to think of my sexuality, because we never had sex. She was okay with that, but I could tell she wanted more. She would linger when we said good-night after an evening together, as if waiting for me to make a move. She never pushed me into a sexual relationship, though. She was passive and compliant, and she was willing to accept my terms, waiting patiently, even though she was in love with me.

So we had a great friendship instead, which Jodi accepted. But by the time senior year rolled around—and the next stage in my life became a closer reality—I began to rethink our friendship. I was so methodical, so programmed in my thinking about life, that I thought my great friend, Jodi, would in fact make the perfect wife for the perfect life. She had been in love with me all those years, and when we began dating again toward the end of our four years at Northwestern, she was very happy, and I believed I was on my way to the life I had always dreamed of.

Four

The Family Business

There's a time to learn and a time to earn. I eventually reached my time to earn. I was twenty-two years old, tall and skinny and motivated to start my lifelong dream of happily ever after. I wanted a fulfilling job and a gratifying, loving family, and I was willing to do whatever it took to achieve my dream.

I decided to try to earn my living on Broadway. I knew it was a long shot, but my passion for the stage ran deep, and I thought I had what it took. I had drive, wit, willingness to work hard, and an unquenchable hunger for theater. I never wanted to be an actor because I had terrible stage fright. I wanted to be a producer, aspiring to no less than the success of some of my greatest idols, Oscar Hammerstein, Richard Rogers, and Hal Prince.

So I made a deal with my parents. Unlike my two older brothers, who were already working in the family business, I would give my dream a try before making any other career decisions. I got an internship in theater management with the Shubert Organization in New York and lived at home while I applied myself to the task. I took the Long Island Railroad into Penn Station every day, joining an army of Long Island commuters on their daily haul.

It didn't take long before I figured out that the backstage theatrical work I had devoted myself to in high school and college was nothing like the grind as a production intern in New York. When I got up in the morning, I dreaded the day ahead and worried that my dream was turning into a nightmare. I filed huge amounts of paperwork, answered the phones, tracked down missing or late set equipment and materials, and sometimes had absolutely nothing to do at all. The tasks were custodial, mundane, and stiflingly boring. Getting coffee for others was a highlight of the day—it got me out of the cramped offices above the dark theater for a shot of daylight.

One day, I met a producer who'd come to see my boss, who was notorious for being late for all his meetings. We fell into a conversation while he waited, and he recognized me for the Broadway wannabe I was. Or maybe he was just in the mood for some conversation while he killed time. He was a real caricature of a Broadway producer—short and pudgy, with a twitchy manner, a strong New York accent, and a big cigar. He wore a rumpled suit, a stained tie loosely knotted around his neck, and sported long, bushy, salt-and-pepper sideburns that were a throwback to the seventies.

"Hey, kid," he said. "Why don't you go for coffee and bring one for me, will ya? I'm tired, and I could use a shot of caffeine. Get one for yourself while you're at it." He pulled a rumpled wad of cash out of his pants pocket and tossed me a twenty.

"Sure," I said, always glad for the break. "There's a diner right around the corner."

I liked him right away for his straightforward New York friendliness and his seeming nonchalance with the money. I hustled out for the coffee and brought it back fast.

"You're quick, kid. I like that. Shows you don't waste time. Take a load off your feet. Don't worry if they get mad at you for loafing around. I'll vouch for you."

He took all the extra sugar packets in the bag and poured them into his coffee. I had thrown in quite a few extras, just in case. I sat down and took the other coffee, even though I hated coffee.

"What are you doing here?" he asked. "I can tell you're not an actor, so what's your deal?"

"I'm working here to see if I want to be a producer." I didn't know who he was, but I had the feeling he knew what he was talking about. Maybe he was my ticket out of the Shubert and into something big.

"Oh yeah?" He laughed. "Do ya have a pile of money as big as Fort Knox? A never-ending fountain of hope? How 'bout a death wish? That could come in handy, too."

"Death wish?" This wasn't the response I was expecting.

"Ya want to be a producer? I wanted to be a producer, too. I made a few dollars at first, and I thought I could never fail. But I'm telling ya, I was wrong. I invested a pile of money in a show I thought was a sure smash—*Bring Back Birdie*, the sequel to *Bye Bye Birdie*, one of the biggest hits on Broadway ever. You ever hear of it?"

"Of course."

"You ever hear of the sequel?"

"Well...no."

"There you go. The damn show ran for four days. I lost my shirt, I lost my nerve, and to top it all off, I lost my wife when the money disappeared. You wanna be a producer? Get ready to ride the roller coaster of your life. Your bank account will go up and down more times than a bride's skirt on her honeymoon."

I blinked a bit at his bluster, but given what I'd been seeing backstage, I could easily believe it. I understood that the theater offered a life of spectacular highs and lows that a risk-averse person like myself would find terrifying. My family had always been generous, but my brothers and I were taught the value of a dollar with weekly allowances and Saturday jobs. High-risk investments were not part of that work ethic. A reliable income and security made houses, wives, and children and a stable way of life possible. I wanted all that badly.

And I clearly wasn't going to get it in the theater.

My father's standing invitation to join the costume jewelry business and work with him and my brothers grew more and more appealing. I was needed in sales, and I knew I would be good at that. I would also have the opportunity to travel widely and to help create a bigger, more successful business. On the other hand, I knew the jokes about sons who joined family businesses. I winced at the idea of people saying behind my back (and sometimes even to my face) that I was a member of "the Lucky Sperm Club," literally a below-the-belt jab at my self-esteem.

But the family business would provide me with the financial security that would enable me to have the life I always wanted. I could get married, support a family, and I could pursue my love of theater as a volunteer or a patron of the arts, rather than yet another neurotic, desperate producer.

So one evening, I heard myself say to my parents at the dinner table, "I'm thinking of joining the family business after all, when the internship ends."

"Good," my father said, without lifting his eyes as he cut his steak. "We're leaving for Providence, Rhode Island, tomorrow. I need you to come with me."

And that was it. My father had never acknowledged that I might not join the business during my first days out of college. He never said to me, "It's your choice, Richard. Try what you love." He was a product of his own generation, a man who was in the US Coast Guard during the Korean War, gladly returning home to safety and security and the business his father had started. He thought the idea of choosing a risky career in the theater industry was frivolous, if not absurd, when the opportunity to join a thriving, viable company was available.

As I debated the decision to join the family business, I comforted myself with one thought. I knew in this one, critical area, he actually needed me. Although I had always felt an uncomfortable, unspoken distance between us, I knew I could do the kind of job my father would appreciate. I told myself over and over again that I was fortunate. I would be able to get an apartment in New York and get started on the life I'd always dreamed of.

In fact, our situation was quite unusual. Each of the family members working there contributed to the business in a different way. Robert worked in the manufacturing arena, Randy in distribution, and we each respected the others' achievements and difficulties. I knew other people who had joined their family businesses, only to find they and their siblings were competing against each other or stepping on one another's toes. Of course, I worried that I had sold out on my dreams, but I buried these thoughts as deeply as my fears about my sexuality. I never uttered a word aloud to anyone about either situation. But I did find other outlets besides work.

Five

Tikkun Olam

I had a good friend from Northwestern University, Rita, whose father, Leonard was a leading social activist. He was a brilliant, spiritual, and kind man, who created Mazon, a Jewish organization dedicated to eradicating worldwide hunger. He cared deeply about the fate of the world and spoke often about each person's responsibility to help others less fortunate. I was lucky to know him and proud that he liked me.

"Richard, what are you doing with your life?" he asked me over dinner when I visited the family in their Boston home. I'd just abandoned the theater, so the question gave me pause.

"You must live intentionally, not throw away your life," he said.

He did not say I was capable of greater things than working in a family costume-jewelry business, but part of me heard that. Many of my friends were on their way to becoming doctors, lawyers, and masters of the universe on Wall Street. But they didn't have a lucrative opportunity waiting for them as I did, nor the long-buried dream of making their parents happy by joining that business.

But I took his words to heart, recommitting myself each time I visited to live a Jewish life, which emphasized Tikkun Olam, acts of kindness performed to perfect or repair the world. It was all part of a bargain I made with myself. I would work with my father and brothers in the business and do the best I could, even if the work was not as glamorous or as professional as what I might have been capable of. I made peace with my choice and resolved never to complain or regret my decision. I was lucky, and I knew it.

I got my first studio apartment in New York on the Upper West Side. I was happy to take all the furniture in my parents' basement and started working at the Walter Heimler Costume Jewelry Company. I worked with two of my brothers and my father, and we got along well. There was no vicious infighting, and I quickly learned the basics of my job. I felt no regret, just anticipation that the decision I made would enable me to make money, see my many friends already in New York, and pursue my outside interests.

I volunteered to work with the elderly again, this time with Volunteers of Yorkville, an agency that helped the elderly who lived in the Yorkville section of New York, which was an old, mostly German neighborhood on the Upper East Side.

They set me up with William Moller. He was not German, but a Danish immigrant in his eighties, who had recently lost his beloved wife. They were married for over fifty years and worked together every day in a Danish food market on Madison Avenue. Their customers were wealthy clients who lived on the most elegant streets of Manhattan's Upper East Side. After his wife died, William was bereft, and I was asked to help him out.

He lived in a miniscule, immaculate studio apartment on Madison Avenue. Besides his bed, a tiny sofa, and a coffee table, the apartment was filled with books and Danish knickknacks. One narrow wall in the apartment housed all the kitchen he needed—a miniature refrigerator and sink and an electric hotplate.

When I arrived the first day, he was surprised.

"I asked for a voman. I vas calling a dating service."

I laughed. "Nope. You got me instead."

Apparently, I was enough. He welcomed me graciously and launched immediately into the story of his life, serving and befriending the most famous residents of Fifth and Madison Avenues at his now defunct Danish market.

"I am vorking for Brooke Astor now," he told me, in his Danish accent, dropping the famous name with obvious relish. In the firmament of wealthy New York society, Brooke Astor was the brightest star. She was a world-famous socialite, a renowned philanthropist, and uniquely, a hands-on volunteer. When William's wife became ill and they had to close the store, he was hired by Mrs. Astor, whose service staff frequented his store and knew him, to clean her monumental silver collection.

"She has a valk-in safe in her apartment filled with silver," he told me.

His tales were always legendary. He knew stories about Nancy Reagan and Betsy Bloomingdale and many of New York's elite, and he loved to share all the gossip.

His favorite outing was to the Metropolitan Museum on Fifth Avenue, though not for the exhibits. He loved sitting inside the museum's great entrance, people-watching, but the museum's suggested admission charge appalled him. No matter that they had some of the greatest art in the world.

"They charge ten dollars to get in!" He was outraged. But he contrived a solution. We would go over, and William would direct me.

"Go in, Richard, and see what color the pins are today."

Upon admission to the Metropolitan Museum, patrons received small, round, colored metal pins to affix to their clothing to prove they had paid the entry fee. William had a plastic bag filled with pins that he had collected over the years, and he would give me the task of finding out the color of the day. When I told him, he would proudly dig through the bag and produce the two pins we needed that day. We affixed them to our shirts and in we would walk, for free, blatantly ignoring the "suggested" donation price for admittance.

William and I remained friends for years. Once, years later, I brought him to my parents' house in Litchfield, Connecticut, for

Thanksgiving dinner. They moved after we all finished college and took our places in the family business, making it possible for my father to retire.

As we pulled off the highway and onto Route 7, and the frenzy of trucks barreling by gave way to rolling hills and the occasional field, he said, "You know, I had a house near here."

"Come on, William," I said. "You were a city boy, through and through. You never lived here."

"No, no, I did. I just never had a chance to tell you. Seriously. That bend that's coming up? Just past it is a yard with a white fence and a huge oak tree. I'm not sure if it's still there, but it used to have a swing hanging from a branch. My house was down the street from there."

Sure enough, as we rounded a bend, there was the tree, still with its swing. And not far beyond, the house he lived in that he had never mentioned.

A few years later, after I was already married to Jodi, I took our son, Michael, to visit William in New York at his apartment. Michael was just about two years old, still in a stroller. William was so delighted to see both of us that he insisted on serving something. He was the worst cook, but the most generous soul, so I hated to refuse him, knowing it would insult him. He made me a cheese sandwich, which was actually inedible. I hid the sandwich in Michael's stroller when he wasn't looking.

William died at ninety-three. In addition to the joy his friendship brought me, my relationship with William taught me one of the most valuable lessons of my young life.

I told a friend about William, including many of the hilarious tales he told me about his life. This friend was a playwright and producer. He used these stories as the basis of *Visiting Mr. Green*, a play he wrote that became one of the longest-running off-Broadway shows ever. William was originally played by the venerable actor Eli Wallach (something that would have made him proud). "My" character was portrayed as a gay man. I was disturbed at being painted as gay on stage and shocked that my supposed friend essentially had stolen my stories without telling me or compensating me in any way. I was twenty-five years old when the play opened. I was newly married, and terrified to make a public or even a private fuss. I went completely underground with the truth.

I had no ability to fight back. I feared exposure or ridicule for being portrayed as gay. I knew I'd been betrayed, and I knew I would have to let it go. It was simply too explosive to confront.

The experience seared me. What I regretted most was my naivete. I'd used my stories to flirt with and impress someone in the theater world who valued them. I'd demeaned myself, offering these tales as evidence of my quirky, interesting, and generous character to someone who took advantage of me. I had failed to protect my own interests. I understood that I had to compartmentalize more tightly than ever anything that would expose me as anything other than heterosexual.

Six

The White Picket Fence

I kept in close touch with all my college friends. Jodi was working in Chicago at her first job in a public relations firm. We spoke on the phone often—long, amusing, and cozy conversations. I knew she was dating a guy in Chicago but was not really committed, either to him or to Chicago. Her family was on the East Coast, and she wanted to come back. I began to fantasize about marrying her. We'd gotten along well at Northwestern. She was vibrant, warm, and loving, with an easygoing personality and a great sense of humor, and I had met her family several times and really liked them as well.

A few months after I began working in the family business, I surprised her. I sent her an airline ticket to New York for Valentine's Day. I included a card saying, "Who knows what will happen?"

I picked her up at Kennedy Airport. In those days, passengers were met at the gate as they came off the airplane. I watched the stream of people coming out of the jet bridge, and then I saw her. She was looking for me, too, confident, but also little vulnerable in the wave of people.

"Richard!" she shouted and waved. She looked very pretty, so happy, and a bit shy, but glad to see me.

I wrapped my arms around her and hugged her, then I kissed her. She was soft and pleasing, her dark hair curled softly around her face in the front and long in the back. I loved her sweetness. I believed she was looking for the same things in life I wanted, and I knew then and there that Jodi would be a wonderful person to live my life with and to have a family with.

I hugged her tightly. I produced a box of chocolates in a heart-shaped box.

She laughed. "Do you remember my favorite? I sure hope there are milk chocolate caramels in there."

It was so easy—so effortless—that it felt right. I couldn't wait to surprise her with the tickets I had gotten to *Dreamgirls*, the hottest show on Broadway.

I took her to dinner at Maxwell's Plum, a chic singles-scene restaurant on the Upper East Side. It was famous for its big-name theater patrons such as Richard Rogers and Barbra Streisand, its Tiffany lamps, and its cachet; and I picked it because I was out to impress her. I knew she actually preferred substance to shine, but I still wanted to show off.

It worked. She felt special and well treated while we dined on expensive hamburgers, and when we spotted the owner, Warner LeRoy, I could tell she felt she had gotten a real New York moment.

When I produced the tickets to *Dreamgirls*, she couldn't take it anymore. "Richard, what are you doing? Are you trying to spin my head around? What's going on with you?"

"I'm planning to convince you to come to New York. So get ready. I promise you I intend to be irresistible."

After dinner, I took her a few blocks away to Peppermint Park, the best ice cream parlor on the east side of New York. We licked our cones despite the February temps and took a cab back to my brother's apartment. He was gone for the weekend, and I had his apartment at my disposal. It was the perfect setup.

We slept together for the first time at my brother's apartment in New York. I knew Jodi was in love with me, and I was convinced I'd found the perfect lifelong companion. I held her and kissed her and made love to her with passion. I felt grateful for her soft and pliant body and did not allow myself thoughts of whether or not the sex was right for me. I convinced myself that we were compatible sexually, which made me very happy. And I wanted more than anything to move in the direction of marriage. I wanted the perfect life, and I believed that with Jodi, I would find it.

We began a long-distance relationship, with me sending her countless cards and frequent gifts. I particularly liked the sexy cards, because they said what I had trouble saying, and it was all easier to say at a distance.

"I keep thinking about your lips," said one.

"Your curves fit my curves," said another.

"You're in my (*inappropriate*) thoughts," was a good one.

"I'm becoming obsessed with you. Watch out!"

"If you think missing me is hard, you should try missing you."

"Admit it, life would be boring without me…"

"I am putting you on my to-do list," said another (that one was probably the most accurate of the bunch).

I knew she had been dating someone in Chicago, and I insisted that she stop seeing him. She had no qualms about it.

But then, over the course of our long-distance relationship, I began to doubt what I was doing. Was I really ready for the commitment I'd led her to believe I wanted? Was she really the perfect girl for me?

I broke up with her again in a long, teary phone conversation. I caught her by surprise, and I really hurt her feelings. She didn't understand my ambivalence. By then, I had become so used to ignoring my attraction for men that I'd never admitted to myself that my sexuality was going to be an issue in our relationship. But I found myself wondering if I was too young, too immature, too inexperienced, or in too much of a hurry.

She came to New York for a visit, and I saw her at a party with all our college friends. She pointedly ignored me and stayed as far away from me as she could. I knew I had hurt her, and I asked myself again what I was doing. I agonized over how cruel my ambivalence had made me. I did love her. I had just been afraid.

I approached her at the party, and she began to cry.

"You know what your problem is, Richard? You are fast and wrong; that's your problem. You love me fast, and then it's wrong. You break up with me fast, and that's wrong. Why don't you figure out what you want? Take your time, and don't call me until you do."

She was shaking, but she meant it. And she was right. I was fast and wrong. Impulsive and cruel. I felt guilty and, worse, stupid. I had found the perfect girl, and I didn't appreciate her. Jodi was everything I had always wanted in a wife: pretty, loving, smart, friendly, popular, generous, and I knew she'd make a great mother...she had it all. She loved her family and had nothing but sweetness in her heart. We always enjoyed each other's company. I couldn't understand what I was doing, and I resolved to correct it.

So I started all over again with the phone calls, the cards, and the gifts. She couldn't resist when I turned on the full charm offensive.

We got engaged when we were both twenty-four years old. A photo of us at our engagement party shows us surrounded by our friends. I look very young and tanned, and I'm smiling broadly, as if I owned the world. I'm wearing a short-sleeved white shirt, a powder-blue vest with a big sailboat embroidered on the left breast, and perfectly creased white linen pants. It never occurred to me that I might look less than 100 percent masculine in that outfit.

We got married in 1985 when we were both twenty-five years old. Our wedding was a great big Jewish splash, planned and paid for by our parents. My only contribution was making up the song list for the wedding, a great long revue of my Broadway favorites. I didn't really understand the lifelong commitment I was making to Jodi or to the words I uttered during our wedding ceremony, but I was happy to be doing what I believed were all the right things.

Jodi was ecstatic. She had fallen in love with me right from the start, and she had gotten her own happily-ever-after dream with the wedding. For our honeymoon, we went to a deluxe hotel in the Caribbean. It seemed like the perfect start.

Jodi landed a job working for a public relations firm in New York, and I was an intrinsic part of the Walter Heimler Costume Jewelry Company. Both of our jobs were mostly nine to five, and we had plenty of time and money for fun, but we started saving for a house right away.

We lived in an Upper East Side apartment. We saw our friends at restaurants, theaters, and sports events such as Jets games and tennis matches, and we frequently made trips to our alma mater, Northwestern, for football games.

Our sex life settled into a pattern. We were vigorous at first but slowed down over time. We really never discussed sex. I assumed she was okay with our lovemaking, because she never complained. Was I passionate? I tried. Was I creative? Probably not.

Was I loyal? Absolutely.

When Jodi gave birth to Michael in 1987, it was one of the happiest moments of my life. I was twenty-seven years old.

I loved Michael with a love I had never experienced before. I was enraptured by everything about him—the smell of him, the weight of him, the sight of him. I carried him around in a little Snuggly that rested on my chest. When he would fall asleep there, I felt a connection so deep it caught me off guard. With the exception of going to work, I was with Michael all the time.

My own father remained distant and distracted, even after I had my son. I thought often about the Harry Chapin song, "Cat's in the Cradle."

"When you coming home, Dad?"

"I don't know when, but we'll get together then, son; we're gonna have a good time then."

I resolved never to have the kind of relationship with my son that I had with my own father. He was certainly there for me when it came to helping me financially, but I never felt a bit of warmth or affection. I saw one of his good friends hug him once, and I saw the bond between them. I couldn't understand why he and I couldn't have that.

I wondered who my father was. His friends said he was a good listener, but it was as if he had a switch he turned off around me. He'd remain stiff, distant, and uncomfortable. His own father, my grandfather, was no better. He was a recluse, living alone in Manhattan. He had started the family costume-jewelry company, and despite the fact that my father had worked with him when we were kids, we did not see him much at all. My sole memory of him is a family outing to a Long Island diner. He came to our house, and we all piled into the car. We drove to the diner in relative silence, compared with our usual boisterous car trips. Somehow, he cast a pall on us all.

In the diner, he barely spoke. I sat next to him, hoping for a bit of attention, a pat on the head, or a question about who I really was. But there was nothing, just an old man with a curved back, gray hair, and a sour look on his face. He endured the meal, in which he said little and showed no interest in me or my brothers.

Jodi's family, on the other hand, was everything I could have asked for. They threw around the "I love yous" freely with each other, and they meant the words. I reveled in that casual, nurturing love whenever I saw them, often remembering my days with my grandmother and grandfather, where the love also flowed freely, with warmth and affection. Jodi's mother, Maxine, treated me like a son, and her father, Lou, was my great friend.

When Michael was born, Lou was overjoyed. They traveled frequently from Philadelphia to see us, and he would lie on the floor playing with Michael for hours, even when he was a baby.

Maxine would say, "Lou, it's time to leave. Tomorrow is a workday."

"What?" he would say, "I can't leave yet. Look; he's just about to figure out how to do this puzzle. I can't miss that!"

Shortly thereafter, we bought a house in Wyckoff, New Jersey, a suburb just a half hour from Manhattan. The house came as close to any dream I ever had about the white-picket-fence life. True,

Life Goes On...Thankfully

there was no picket fence (that metaphor was out of fashion in the suburbs by then), but the house sat invitingly on a green, grassy hill on a quiet, safe street close to the public school and synagogue. We had a big backyard with a pool and room for a swing set and games of touch football and catch. Inside were three bedrooms, an upstairs den, a well-equipped kitchen, and even a large basement that worked as a separate play space for children. Our new Jeep Cherokee sat in a two-car garage at the end of a paved driveway that provided a place to install a basketball hoop for Michael when he was ready. He loved balls from the first day he saw one. No doubt, his uncles' genes.

A new house, a new baby, a charming wife. Trips to England for work, vacations in the Caribbean, ski trips to Vermont, and Broadway shows on weekends. No wonder I completely repressed occasional bursts of my truest sexuality. When I pushed those thoughts aside, I reassured myself that the compromise was worth it, and it certainly seemed to be.

We joined the synagogue, Beth Rishon, and began the process of establishing ourselves there. We took on positions of responsibility and met a host of new friends. Jodi taught part time in the nursery school and became the chairperson of the New Member Committee and then the president of Sisterhood. She was a natural, with her gregariousness and her unstinting inclusiveness. She had a positive aura that drew the many young mothers to her, as they fretted about and shared the responsibilities of raising young children.

She took endless phone calls and answered every manner of question. She made pediatrician, babysitter, and nursery school referrals and began to put together new programs that would bring the women together in the synagogue. We began lifelong friendships with both the rabbi and the cantor.

My contributions were fundraising, programming, and social activism. It took hours and hours, but I loved it. I was doing something important that benefited my family and my religion. I loved being busy and productive and part of a growing synagogue.

When Rachel was born, I felt as if my life was complete. She was a fair and light counterbalance to Michael's dark hair and olive-toned skin, chatty and expansive to his quiet. I felt as if I had it all. A son, a daughter, a wife, a Jewish community, a thriving business, and money enough to travel, visit friends and family, go to the theater, go out to restaurants, and enjoy what life offered.

Rachel was a dream child. Her favorite game was "Let's Pretend." Perhaps she was not so unlike her dad. She wanted nothing more than to be a good girl, facing her world with optimism and sweetness.

We bonded over theater when she was little. Rachel's earliest shows were one-actor affairs in which she was the star. They were hyperlocal productions that she staged in our living room, with me or Jodi as the audience. She created sets with dolls, toys, and costumes and was as comfortable with make-believe as with reality. As she got a bit older, she included her friends in her productions. The shows were quite simple, with titles like *He Loves Me* or *Marry Me*. Sometimes there were disappointments when the lovers argued and flounced away. At all times, the plots were imaginative and engrossing for the young actors who, at the age of four and five, lost themselves fully in the drama of their shows. Sometimes, as I watched her so absorbed by her make-believe world, I cheered for her innocence and rapt belief in fairy tales. I loved her fiercely and wanted nothing more than to fulfill her dreams of happily ever after.

As soon as Rachel was old enough to sit still, I began to take her to the theater. It was our special time. I commenced her education with *Disney on Ice*, then *Cats*, *Beauty and the Beast*, and *The Lion King*.

I sat next to her in the theater, nurturing an appetite that I whetted with Twizzlers. When the theater went dark at the start of the show, Rachel settled down, surrendering to the magic in front of her, happier still to be sitting next to the man she most trusted and adored. Shamelessly, I pressed my advantage; I bought her overpriced memorabilia, glossy magazines, T-shirts, an early copy of the soundtrack for the show. When she got a little bit older, we would walk down the Broadway district side streets, studying the marquees, deciding which shows held the most promise.

"Would you like to see this one?" I asked.

Eyes wide, she'd respond, "Really? Yes!"

And I, the magician, would pull two tickets from a pocket. "Let's go!" I never made it on stage, but I was still a showman.

We both collected *Playbills*, sharing a personal disdain for people who disrespected their *Playbills* by being unimpressed by the significance of the information within and ready to toss the fact-filled digest in the trash at the close of the show—or worse, leave it under their velvet seats as they left the theater.

Years later during a chatty phone call, she said, "Dad, my friends just went to see a show. I saw their *Playbills* in the trash can."

"Philistines! They threw away the Bible. They know not what they do."

My own *Playbill* collection was stored in a series of custom, black, loose-leaf binders with clear plastic sleeves specially cut to perfectly hold a *Playbill*. The *Playbill* collector can leaf through his collection, traversing time and space, recapturing the impact of the show, searing or forgettable, but connecting again with the experience through visible proof that he was there, in the theater, a part of the production by his very attendance.

I did regret that I had neglected to save all my ticket stubs as well, for they would have served to remind me when I went, who I went with, where I sat, and the prices I had paid—details I would have appreciated, in retrospect.

Seven

Fever

Were there cracks all along? I suppose there were, but I tried to operate an airtight storage facility, compartmentalizing my homosexuality behind steel doors. Somehow, though, my growing awareness that I was not living my true life leaked through them.

Some people cry in cars when they drive alone, releasing emotion they can't access during the course of everyday living. I let myself go in a darkened theater. Perhaps this was part of my compulsion to return to the theater again and again, despite the high cost of tickets and the travails of traveling to Manhattan's most inhospitable streets. I sat in crowded theaters and uncomfortable seats without complaint. None of it meant anything to me compared with the opportunity to find a meaningful connection with my deepest feelings, my truest self, whether I experienced joy or fear or love or larger thoughts of what my life really meant.

Appropriately enough, the first serious crack in the façade of my life struck me in the theater. I was thirty-two years old. Michael and Rachel were four and two years old, respectively. Jodi and I went to the theater with her parents to celebrate Jodi's birthday. The show was *Falsettos*. It was 1992.

When I sat in the theater that evening next to my wife and her parents, whom I cherished and whose devotion to each other was a source of nourishment in my life, I could not deny that the story about a man who leaves his wife and young son for another man terrified me. I had a flash of recognition, a lightning bolt of understanding in which the thought, "My God, that's me!" entered my mind. I saw my own life, in all its brilliant angst and possibility, right there onstage.

The leading man had married a Jewish woman whose love and commitment he required, but he was in love with another person—a gorgeous and sexual man. His wife perceived that something was lacking in the marriage, but she chose not to admit it. The leading man had fallen in love and was cheating on his wife, which I recognized as wrong but also understood at my core.

Nevertheless, I refused to go from deeply disturbed to honest. I refused to allow the impact of the show to penetrate my conscious experience for too long. I could not entertain that sort of cataclysmic honesty. I clung to the life I had crafted, reminding myself it was all I'd ever dreamed of.

I kept on with my fast-paced life. I had two young children, endless social engagements with Jodi, a gratifying leadership role in the synagogue, and work that required business trips to Europe and the West Coast.

Traveling was one of my favorite parts of the job, and Jodi resented it. Of course, she did. Who wouldn't?

"Jodi," I said. "Sorry to break this to you, but I have to go for London for five days."

She looked at me wearily. "Give me a break. You stay here with the kids, and I'll go to London. I'll meet with the buyers, show them the products, and take them out to dinner and a show, and stay in a nice hotel with room service. Then when I get home, I'll tell you I'm tired and have jet lag."

We both knew it was far easier to get on a plane than to stay home with two little kids. But Jodi didn't know there was a part of the trip she couldn't imagine.

After I saw *Falsettos*, something inside me broke down. Somehow, I knew that the next time I was away, I would do something dangerous. In London, far from home and any accidental connections with my "real" life, I went to a men's public bath late at night. The bathhouse I chose was near the theater district, and I had noticed gay men entering and exiting many times.

I told myself I would not do anything if I went inside. I would just sit there and watch to see what it was like.

I paid my admission and received a white towel, a locker key, and a package of condoms. The attendant was young, lean, muscular, and handsome. I entered, not knowing what to expect.

To my surprise, the place was very clean. I put my belongings and the condoms inside a metal locker and got undressed. I walked bare chested and barefoot into a large and open public space, wrapped in my white towel and nothing else. There was an open area for showering, with no doors for privacy. Several men were lathering up in the open. There was a very large hot tub, with a clean, tiled ledge around the edge. Two men were perched there sitting close to each other, their hands under the water.

I took a shower quickly and walked over to the hot tub. I lowered myself into the water. It was hot and clear, and I sniffed the faint smell of chlorine, which somehow reassured me. The men who had been there were gone. I watched as a few more men entered the room, looked around and checked each other out. The steam room was nearby, and I could see the steam escape as one man entered through a glass door. He did not come out.

I watched as two well-built men went together from the shower area to a small private room on the perimeter. Some doors to the numerous private spaces were shut, but some were left open, an invitation for others to get turned on by watching. These two entered one of the rooms and closed the door. In another room, I saw a man lying on a bed on his back, just waiting. As I watched, someone entered the room and kissed him and then lay down on top of him.

I was nearly unable to control my excitement, but I was terrified to speak with or join anyone. I just stayed in the hot tub.

Life Goes On...Thankfully

A man wearing his own white towel approached me. He was older than me, muscular, and middle-of-the-road handsome. "I've never seen you here before," he said with a British accent. "You're quite adorable. Perhaps this is my lucky night." He sat at the edge of the hot tub, not getting in.

I could scarcely breathe. I laughed, trying to be cool. "Not so lucky. I'm just visiting."

"Ahhh..." he said. "An American, being a tourist. Perhaps I can convince you to change your mind and join us locals."

He moved his towel to open it, revealing a large erect penis. I immediately noticed that he had a foreskin, which surprised me—all the men I knew were circumcised. So, not a good Jewish boy. I almost laughed at my weird reaction.

"No thanks. Just sightseeing."

"Too bad. If you change your mind, I'll be in that room back there." He pointed to a room where two men were having sex with the door open.

I sat there in the hot tub, unable to believe I was actually crossing this line. He was a total stranger, but I was drawn to joining him, despite my better judgment. In fact, the temptation was almost overwhelming. Who would know? But I held on to my fear and denial, reminding myself that these were total strangers, and asking myself what I would do if anyone tried to hurt me, or follow me, or steal my wallet. And what if I did have sex with one of these men? Could I get an STD?

I remembered the condoms in my locker.

I was terrified of what could happen and of what I was doing. I'd gone to the bathhouse to see what it would be like...and, to be honest, to find out if I would be attractive to anyone. Now I knew how easy it could be.

I stayed in the hot tub a while longer, watching, with a feeling of longing I had never experienced before. Finally, I left and went back to my hotel, exhausted. I had resisted the temptation, but I had broken a barrier, and I knew it.

Once back in my hotel, I told myself that no one knew I did this, and I forced myself to put it out of my mind as soon as I got home.

~

A year later, I saw *La Cage aux Folles*.

A big, bold Broadway musical and a smash hit, it told the story of a flamboyant gay couple who pretend to be straight for one night for the sake of their son, who was in love with a girl with a homophobic father. The hit song in the show was, "I Am What I Am." The song became a gay anthem, and when the star, Harvey Fierstein, outrageous and unapologetic, finished the number, all the gay men in the audience threw their *Playbills* in the air. I wanted so badly to throw mine up in the air as well, but I couldn't join them because I was with Jodi. But inside, I was cheering as loud as I could.

My happiness did not last long. How could it? Happiness that you have to keep secret might be pleasurable for some, but not for me. When I'm happiest, I want to share it with those around me, not keep deep secrets buried inside. Shouldn't love be an experience that we share and take joy from?

Soon after that, I saw *Miss Saigon*. I fell immediately and obsessively in love with the star, Sean McDermott. He was tall, dark-haired, and slender with the most captivating face and voice. I was simply overwhelmed. I didn't know what to do with my feelings. I saw the show four times just to see him again and again. Each time I went to see the show, I craved him more.

Usually I went to the theater with family or business associates. But this was different. I wanted to be alone as I watched him, without distraction. I lied about where I was going to Jodi, because I knew she wouldn't understand. How could she? I could barely understand it, myself.

After the fourth time I saw the show, I waited by the stage door to see him come out, just like a teenage groupie. Another night, unable to escape from my obsessive fantasies, I didn't attend the show, but I went to the stage door and waited for him to come out. I followed him. In truth, I stalked him. I wanted to know where he was going, what he was doing, and where he lived. I had fantasies that if I just introduced myself to him, he would fall in love with me at first sight.

I could not fathom what was happening to me. I could no longer control my mind or my actions. It was the first time my desire moved from the back burner to the front. Previously, I'd exercised some sort of magical thinking that enabled me to turn away from the urges within. But the obsession I had for this man could not be controlled. It was urgent, irresistible, and primal. It did not feel good.

Finally, terrified that I might do something I would regret, I forced myself to stop. I needed to regain control. No more tickets to the show and no more visits to stage door.

Eight

A Raging Fire

Y2K was the first day of the new millennium, January 1, 2000. It was a frightening time. Experts were predicting a worldwide collapse of electricity and communications. The president of the United States, Bill Clinton, warned that it was one of the most complex management crises in history. The news was filled with stories about people setting up underground bunkers, stocking up on canned foods, and staying home for the usually busy Christmas and New Year's holidays. It was hard to know what to believe. Could the world as we knew it really be ending?

Like many of our worst fears, Y2K was overblown. There was no debacle. The fixers had outrun the fearmongers. In fact, so much preparation had been done in anticipation of the problem that there was no problem at all. Could I take heart from this? Was it possible that I might be able to figure out a way to avoid this disaster I feared so intensely?

Jodi and I both turned forty during the millennium. For this milestone in our lives, we had a big splashy party in New York, surrounded by friends and family. It appeared we had the life everyone envied, elegant and festive. Of course, I wrote a speech. Just after I read my birthday accolades to Jodi, feting her and our life together at this milestone, a friend and neighbor, in the throes of a divorce, approached me.

"You know," she said, "you didn't once look at Jodi while you read your speech."

Her words jolted me. No matter how hypersensitive she might have been, while caught up in the sorrow and anger of her own dissolving marriage, I believed she detected something real, something rotten—an unwillingness on my part to fully embrace the words and the moment. I could not repress my growing awareness that my sexuality was becoming an issue I could not ignore.

The big party over, we returned to the silvery gloss of our privileged lives.

But there was a new distraction. Technology had burst upon the scene and was a growing part of our existence. Cell phones were everywhere, there was a computer on everyone's desk, and all the new equipment was becoming easier to use and more affordable. Like so many others, I was captivated. The internet was exploding with possibilities of communication I had never dreamed of. I got a "handle" and a screen name.

And a new secret identity.

I began to explore websites where my own private secrets and fears about my sexuality were being openly discussed. In short order, I became an addict. And like so many addicts, I lied to myself. I told myself I was doing no harm, just reading, but it was clear that the more I read, the more I wanted to read. I would get online at work when my brothers were out to lunch or away from the office. I slipped out of bed at night when Jodi fell asleep and logged on in our den, carefully closing the door so I would know if she woke up and came looking for me.

Then, on September 11, 2001, the World Trade Center was attacked, and it looked as if the world was ending.

All over the country, people were stunned, shocked, and dislocated, but New York was my town, and the ramifications of the disaster shook me profoundly. Because of our proximity to the World Trade Center, we all knew someone who had lost a loved one or actually died in the disaster. That sudden awareness of our mortality also crept into my being. Three thousand people dead. So many lives shattered in an instant. I read their stories each morning in the newspaper in the months that followed. They were everyday people, mourned by their loved ones. The stories about married men, gay men in partnered relationships, and single people hit me particularly hard.

I was more and more uncomfortable with the idea that I was not living my true life, even though I told myself that I had everything I' ever dreamed of. I couldn't seem to put the genie back in the bottle.

~

A few months later, Jodi and I had dinner in Manhattan with Henry and Margie, our college friends. I had been to Margie's home in Philadelphia many times, and I knew her parents well. Her father was a self-assured, successful lawyer with a big ego, and her mother was a stay-at-home mom who had raised Margie and her two sisters. She remained devoted to her family, often taking trips to babysit for her grandchildren.

With tears brimming in her eyes, Margie told us that her parents had nearly divorced. "My father had a year-long affair with one of my parents' bridge partners. My mother became suspicious after my father started coming home late, and when he came home he was distant and short-tempered. When she questioned him about the unusual frequency of the business dinners, he erupted at her. The change was so abrupt that she felt something was wrong. Finally, she confronted him and asked if he was having an affair. At first he denied it, then he admitted it. He said they hadn't had any kind of satisfying sex in years, and that the woman loved him and made him feel like a real man again.

"It was cheap and tawdry and so utterly humiliating to my mother," said Margie.

Life Goes On...Thankfully

They lived in the house together, not speaking until they separated. It was only after their adult children convinced them to resume their forty-five-year marriage that they got back together.

I pictured a relationship in which two people cohabited, but with the love and trust gone forever. One day would I be sixty-five-years old and still dealing with my sexual temptation? At the sunset of my life, would I still be worrying that I had to experience my true sexuality before the final tick of the clock? Would I become a closeted cheater, forever worried I would be caught in duplicitous and humiliating sexual encounters with men?

I was shaken by a vision that flashed in front of me, a crystal ball that indicated I would be faced with a terrible, inevitable choice: my own sexuality or truth and the destruction of my family.

The restaurant was lovely. The food was top-notch. It all meant nothing to me, and I pushed my plate away, wondering what would become of us all.

~

Shortly thereafter, while sitting at my desk in my office, supposedly working, I discovered a website called Closed Loop. It wasn't a sex website, but rather a place for men who were questioning their own sexuality. There were 23,000 members in the New York area alone. It was dizzying.

I scanned the data bank and found married guys of every stripe. Guys of all ages. Guys in open marriages, guys who loved their wives more than life itself, guys with children, guys with grandchildren, guys whose wives knew their secret, guys who had never told a soul. Guys right near me, from New York; guys from New Jersey; and guys from Massachusetts. Guys who were looking for friendship, guys who were looking for a "buddy" for regular sexual encounters. I was riveted.

I met a man named Lee online. He had a wife, two children. He was funny, he was closeted, and he was trapped. He was me.

"Are you my blood brother?" I asked him. "Were we separated at birth?"

It was as if I'd been alone in the wilderness and then suddenly got water, food, company. I couldn't get enough of him. We emailed back and forth obsessively. All of a sudden, I could live it, talk about it. It was intoxicating.

When we connected online, I was crazed. My heart would race, and I'd be riveted by his words. I let my calls go unanswered and skipped important appointments if I was online with him. I couldn't wait for the next contact. There was an infatuation to it. I was trying to keep my life normal, but I was far from normal. I couldn't think straight.

I would chat with him online for a while, and then, like a drug addict I'd swear I would stop. As soon as a little time went by, the familiar cravings returned. I couldn't wait to check my messages, couldn't wait for the next connection to pump me up. The communication felt cathartic. We shared the same pain, the same anxiety, the same thoughts.

Unlike Jodi, Lee's wife was suspicious and confrontational. So much of Lee's energy was spent hiding his obsessions from her, fearful that she would somehow intuit his desperation.

Then, catastrophe. "The thing I was most afraid of has just happened," he wrote in an online chat. "I've just been outed by my wife."

Suspecting something was awry, Lee's wife clicked the "history" tab on his computer, revealing his visits to a long list of gay websites. She opened the Closed Loop website, read as much as she could stand, and confronted her husband. She was raging. As I read his words, I shivered. I feared for myself all over again.

"It was every bit as awful as I ever thought it would be to be discovered," he wrote. "She threatened to take my kids away from me. She told me I was the worst liar and the most dishonest, disgusting person. She said she was ashamed that I was the father of her children. She said she would tell them I was a faggot and I had betrayed them all. I was crying so hard...I told her I'd never meant to harm her, that I was sorry I hurt her so desperately. I told her I never cheated on her, just went online and explored but never ever betrayed her.

"To be honest," he admitted, "sometimes I did wish for this nightmare to be over, imagining that anything would be better than the torture I experienced hiding who I really am. But I was wrong. The thought of losing my kids and being exposed publicly was worse. I'll never forget her screaming and crying. She actually took off her wedding ring and threw it at me. She kept carrying on and on. 'We built a life together based on your lies. The whole thing is a lie! You are unimaginably vile!'"

In each email he sent me after that, his pain was evident. His wife threatened to take the kids away, but ultimately, he promised he would never leave her or them, and she believed him. They decided to stay together. Shortly after that, he stopped responding to my messages. I never found out how it all ended.

~

I would sit at my desk, doing no work at all, perusing the internet for longer and longer stretches. Unexpectedly one day, my brother came into my workspace, and I had to quickly move off a gay website. It seemed he didn't notice it, but I panicked.

By day, I lived my life as a family man, never giving away the growing distraction I could no longer fend off. My wife did not know. My children were oblivious. Their happiness had always been my first concern, but now I counted on their immersion in their own lives to prevent them from seeing that I was exploring a new direction.

Then I met Gary.

I met him on a website called Gay.com, a site for men who wanted anonymous same-day sex. I was in the New York City chat room, scanning the profiles and names of each of the guys currently chatting. I clicked on one called "outreach13" because the mini bio read "divorced soccer dad, 40." He was from a suburb of Philadelphia and was a gay divorced dad with three young children.

We hit it off online. Every day, I'd send him an email. Some of my questions were silly, such as, "what baseball player do you think is sexy?" but many were about real life. I asked how his kids were dealing with his situation. I learned that he'd never told his family he was gay. He was divorced but never told his family the truth. I was a complete stranger to him, but he confided everything about his own experience. He was my mentor. Every day, he took the time to respond to the email I sent him. He took all my calls. I started to fall in love with him even though I had never met him. My computer offered the seductive promise of both anonymity and entrée to a whole new world. I told him my deepest secrets.

"I am currently struggling with two issues," I wrote in an instant message. "First is my sexuality. I've known I like men forever, but it was on the back burner for many years. Now these 'bi' thoughts are percolating, and I've decided to see what is really going on. I am not sure what I'll do if I am really honest with myself, but it's time to take this journey.

"My other issue is my love for my wife. I'm not sure I love her enough to be with her forever and ever. I love the life we have built, and I love her for being an outstanding companion and friend for many years. But I'm not sure I'm in love with her anymore. It's very unsettling when you cannot completely be yourself or give all your love to your life partner. I am so concerned that if we separate because of me, all the good that I've done with my kids over the last fifteen years will be wiped out in five minutes."

Once I had given voice to my feelings, I was overwhelmed with wanting. I could no longer compartmentalize, rationalize, or deny. I was tantalized by the nearness of the life I wanted to live, though terrified of losing the people that I cherished. The way forward—into a new life—had once seemed inconceivable to me. But it was beginning to seem like a possibility, because it was becoming clear there was no road back. I did have the choice to somehow bury this powerful urge within me, but I could not imagine how I would bear the suffering that would entail. I was determined to figure out a way. The decision to try to move forward—the thought that perhaps I could figure out how to be true to myself *and* stay true to my loved ones—was energizing. This was my first thought every morning and my last thought at night.

From my desk at work, I wrote an email to Gary.

"Sometimes I wish I could have a 'time-out' like we give our kids. I need to figure out what I've done wrong, and what I can do to fix it, and set things right again. But there is no time-out. I am here on this journey in uncharted waters. But I am determined to find a way somehow. I have been so lucky in my life. Dare I dream I can create a new path and not lose the people I love and who love me? I have no illusions. I know the way would be calamitous in the beginning, but I also want to believe that I can find a happy ending, despite the odds and despite my fears.

"I believe that there are magical relationships out there and that maybe I too can be a part of one. I have so much love to give, and I realize now I am no longer capable of giving my wife the kind of love she deserves. I probably will never have 100 percent happiness and contentment in my life because no matter what road I choose, I'll always have some regrets and pain. But now I want to strive for the most happiness and inner peace that is possible with the foundation of my life already cemented. Is it my time now?"

I couldn't help myself any longer. I wanted a love I could jump through fires for. I permitted myself the realization that deep down, I did not love my wife with all my heart. I dreamed of a kind of love in which there were no secrets, a romantic love in which I could say with all my heart and body, I love you. Was my yearning for a new start just another Broadway script where the lead character was doomed from the beginning? I hoped not.

I felt the inevitability of the decision. I wanted to protect Jodi and my children, even as I was about to destroy their lives. It was up to me to make that transition as courageously as I could. I knew that if I continued on this torturous path, I would eventually expose them to something shameful, but if I took matters into my own hands, perhaps I could influence the outcome so that by some miracle, we would have a chance for a happy ending.

I was also very frightened.

Every year, we spent a long weekend at the beach in Montauk, Long Island, with a group of our best friends from Wyckoff. We all knew each other well after years in the synagogue and endless hours on sports fields and at weekend birthday parties for our kids.

In the summer of 2002, I could barely face our annual outing. For the first time ever, I felt uncomfortable with my friends, who even commented that I seemed quiet and reserved. I was sleeping poorly, and the days felt endless. I didn't want to be around anyone who knew me, and most especially, I didn't want to be alone in the hotel room with Jodi. Our sex had become mechanical and repetitive, but she seemed not to notice or care. We never discussed it. Every time I was with her now, I felt reminded of a life I no longer wanted to live. My life had become a charade.

Finally, I lied to her.

Nine

You Can Sing a Different Song

"I might have to leave, Jodi. I just got a call from my brother. There's a problem at work. A client in London is threatening to cancel a major sale, and if that happens, I'll have to fly over there to try to resurrect the account."

It was a glib lie, and it was surprisingly easy. Jodi believed every word. We were in our motel room in Montauk, and I could not stay for one more second.

"That's too bad!" she said. "I hope you don't have to ruin your time here, but if you have to go, you'll just have to drive to the airport, and I'll get a ride home."

She didn't mind. She was surrounded by friends who would take care of her in my absence, and not once did she doubt me or my loyalty.

But I was no longer trustworthy. I was changing. Everything was in disarray. Unrecognizable parts of me were suddenly brazen and bold. Parts of me still held fast to the old me, but the hold was loosening, and my thoughts had turned to obsessions.

I was no longer in control. I craved interaction with Gary. He was the first person I had encountered with whom I could be my new self. I could say anything to him. He understood everything I said. I could not imagine going through this experience without him. I was besotted with him.

Once I'd lied to Jodi, I felt a measure of relief. I'd bought myself some breathing room. I didn't give in to my impulse to leave, but I began making excuses to get off the beach to check my emails, ostensibly to see if my manufactured crisis was worsening, but really to see if Gary had replied to my last communiqué. I found reasons to go into town and sit in parking lots, waiting for his next phone call. In the middle of it all, I emailed Gary a list of my sins, a chronicle of my betrayals, couched in flirtatious and self-deprecating humor.

Top Ten Reasons You Know Your Marriage Is Over:
10. You are relieved when your wife has her period each month.
9. While playing Boggle with your wife at the beach, you are busy checking out the other dads building sand castles with their kids.
8. At the mall, you find yourself walking in front of the Abercrombie & Fitch or Hollister stores, checking out the eighteen-year-old, shirtless guys on the posters.
7. You would rather watch *Six Feet Under* in the basement to follow the gay character's story line than *West Wing* in the den with your wife (even though Rob Lowe is a hottie also).
6. In a restaurant, you hope your wife goes to the bathroom so you can twist off your wedding band and have a conversation with the hot waiter.
5. While making love with your wife, you wonder, *Does she know what I'm thinking?*
4. On a business trip in another city, you go to the Gay and Lesbian section at Barnes and Noble to check out the books and the guys in that aisle.
3. You allow your daughter to watch *The Real World*, even though it is past her bedtime, so you can see the hot guys on the show.
2. You go to Blockbuster to pick a movie to watch with your wife. She picks a sexy movie with Penelope Cruz, but you overrule her for a very violent *Black Hawk Down* just because Josh Hartnett is in it.

Life Goes On...Thankfully

1. When Cher sings "Is There Life after Love?" you want to say, "I hope so." And when she sings, "Sooner or Later, We All Sleep Alone," you say, "I know it, and I am prepared to."

~

When the interminable weekend was finally over, Jodi and I drove home from the beach together. I didn't leave for the manufactured crisis in Europe, but I decided I had to speak with her truthfully. There was no one in the car but the two of us for the three-hour drive to New Jersey. The traffic was still light, but I knew it would build as we left the relative quiet of Montauk and made our way west through the glamour towns, East Hampton, Bridgehampton, Sag Harbor, Wainscott, and Southampton until we hit the Long Island Expressway. That two-lane road, which was built to handle traffic of a bygone era, was choked, but it was the only way back.

Jodi sat next to me, a bit sunburned and tired after our last day at the beach. Her dark hair was pulled back in a ponytail, and she wore a baseball cap that said, "Life's a beach."

I kept my eyes on the road ahead, afraid to look at her. I began to speak the words I had rehearsed in my head over and over again.

"Jodi, I know you must be wondering why I've been acting so strangely. I'm so sorry to tell you this, but I'm not in love with you anymore."

I breathed. I pressed on. I would not stop, even though I could feel my words cutting straight through to her sweet heart and kind, innocent soul.

"There is nothing you can do to make this any different, and you did not do anything wrong, but I think that we might have to separate. It's not about anything you did, it's about me, and I can't tell you why."

Stunned and not comprehending, she looked at me. Of all the things I ever said when I was sad or frustrated or annoyed or angry, I had never uttered such words to her before. It was unthinkable to her. It was a language she did not understand, a sledgehammer of unexpected cruelty from the person she had always trusted.

Jodi was a crier. Angry, sad, happy, or simply moved, her emotional response to the best and the worst was always tears. Sure enough, her eyes began to well up, her nose to redden, and her next response, also painfully predictable, was to assume she had done something wrong—something that she could fix. She immediately sought a way to eradicate the words I had just spoken, to pretend they had never been said; or at the very least, to come up with a workable solution to this outrageous, unpredictable, inconceivable problem that suddenly swept her up like a sandstorm.

"What have I done?" she asked. "Is it sex? Is it too much, too little, too boring, too mechanized, too routine after seventeen years of marriage? Am I too fat, too predictable? Is it too much family? Is it too many obligations with the children? Do you need more time with your friends and less time with me?"

She was bargaining, trading in my words for a problem with a solution—or at least a viable means of covering up the ugly, unacceptable vision of the future I had just placed before her.

I felt sick, but I was determined. I stared at the cars in front of me without looking at her. I gave her no answers. I just kept repeating, "It's not you. It's me. I can't tell you why. I think I might need a separation to think things through."

It was the best I could do. I could do nothing more in that moment. We passed the rest of the car ride home in silence. She looked out the window, and the glass reflected her tears.

~

My guilt was tremendous. She had promised me her love forever, and when I asked her to marry me, she expected the same. And even though I didn't have a master plan that included getting married and having kids and then waking up one day to live life as

Life Goes On...Thankfully

a gay man, I always knew that I didn't love Jodi the way she loved me.

In my most desperate thoughts, I sometimes wished I were the kind of coward who'd made her complicit in my behavior. At the age of twenty-five, I could have said, "I love you, Jodi, and I want to share my life with you. But you need to know I have always had a secret attraction to men that I think won't affect our marriage."

I believe Jodi still would have married me, and if I had verbalized those thoughts then, at least my guilt would be less. But I could never have uttered those words. And even if I had, even if I had forced her to collude with me, would it have made me feel any less responsible? Probably not. I probably would have hated myself for forcing her to compromise her own life's dream.

We lived in a state of torment for the next few weeks, going through the familiar motions of our lives but hardly speaking to each other. Our kids went on with their lives oblivious to our emotional dislocation. All the while, I continued my endless forays on the internet. There was no way back from the course I was steering.

Our den had a wall of bookcases where we kept our voluminous photo album collection. The collection contained thousands of snapshots documenting the best days of our lives. I'd organized it, so it was labeled with dates and titles, making it easy to reference birthdays, anniversaries, and celebrations not only in our lives but in those of our families and friends. The albums were a reference library for my oft-stated life belief in the importance of "making memories."

Our desktop computer was in the den, as well. One day, I was planning to make a surreptitious foray to my usual gay websites when Jodi entered the room. I waited for her to leave so I could go back to my internet surfing, but she had a different agenda.

"I'm going to find some photo albums we can use to make a video for Rachel's Bat Mitzvah," she announced, and she began poking around the bookshelves, looking for some albums of the kids when they were little. Of course, we had tons of albums, thanks to my obsession with recording every milestone in their lives, and she pulled a few heavy volumes off the shelves. Her arms loaded, she dropped a heavy, three-ring binder on her foot and yelped in pain.

"I think I broke my toe!" she cried, kneeling down and rubbing her bare foot.

"What's the matter with you? Why aren't you wearing shoes?" I asked, steaming because her presence in the den prevented me from getting online. I got up, left the room, and went to sit out by the pool.

Several minutes later, she limped out to the pool. She was angry. "What is wrong with you?" she demanded. "What kind of ridiculous reaction is that? I tell you I think I broke my toe, and you act like I'm bothering you?"

Instantly, I felt guilty. I had hurt her for no reason except my own selfishness. But I took the opportunity to move my agenda forward.

"Jodi," I said. "I don't think I can love you the way you need to be loved."

She looked at me, torn, caught in a no-win situation. She wanted to go on with our lives as if the cracks had never surfaced, and I was not acquiescing. She turned on her good foot and left the pool without a word.

Just a couple of weeks later, we were once again at the beach, this time with Jodi's family in Margate, New Jersey. Jodi's sister, Beth, was one of the few people Jodi had confided in about the lightning bolt I had hurled at her and our lives. Beth and I had always been terrific friends. I knew she was devoted to Jodi, and if I hurt Jodi, I would risk losing Beth in my life. We took a walk on the beach, and she wasted no time.

"Richard, of course Jodi's told me that you are both in the middle of a crisis, but she hasn't been able to tell me more. You know I love you and don't want to hurt you, but I think I know what's wrong. Are you gay? Because if that's the reason, please let's talk about it. We can be honest with each other."

Life Goes On...Thankfully

There it was. Truthfulness. Honesty. Bravery. The warmth and love I had always been lucky enough to receive from Jodi's mother, father, and sister. I felt a small surge of gratitude, a harbinger of hope. Maybe the people I knew and loved so well—and who loved me right back—were searching for a rationale for my behavior and a workable solution to the crisis I'd created.

I could not yet deal with the thought that perhaps I had been blind. Perhaps those who knew and loved me had suspected I was gay long before I was ready to face the truth. Anyway, it didn't matter. What mattered now was that I had entered into a lifelong contract that I was about to violate. No matter how much I hated myself for that violation, I was unable and unwilling to go back.

"I can't talk about it, Beth." My resistance was maddening, I knew, but I could not speak the words yet. Certainly, I would never tell Beth that I was gay before I told Jodi. But it was a breakthrough. Clearly, Beth already knew my truth. There was kindness in her question and a sign that perhaps—just perhaps—my betrayal would be understood as something I could no longer control.

That spark of kindness from Beth, and the loyalty she showed me, gave me the courage I needed to think clearly. I had been frozen, unsure how to proceed, but after that walk on the beach, I made my plan of action.

~

Henry and Margie, our friends from college, had for years been locked in an unhappy marriage. Margie and Henry's fights and makeup sessions were legendary. She was very open about them to both Jodi and me. There was never a call to the police, but Henry had a short fuse and a creative vocabulary. He was often verbally abusive. He had all the money, too, and that left Margie vulnerable and frustrated. They would make up by taking exotic trips to Tahitian beaches or Italian seaports on the Mediterranean, or they'd go on safari in Africa.

One day, Henry came right out and said he was gay, and he left his family. It seemed as if he emerged unscathed.

Henry knew Jodi and our children very well. We had all seen each other many times over the years since our college days. Their pictures were scattered throughout my photo library.

Henry's was the voice of experience I needed at that moment. I needed reassurance that if he could do it, I could do it. He was the only man I knew personally (not from the internet chat rooms) who had actually blown up his life and come out publicly. And he had not only survived his coming out, but he had flourished. He made it look, if not easy, at least surmountable.

I met Henry at a restaurant in New York's theater district called Vice Versa (yes, that really is the name of the restaurant we picked). He was the first person in my real life with whom I would share my secret.

Even as I walked to the restaurant to meet him, I was telling myself to switch directions, to walk over to the Port Authority Bus Terminal, hop the bus to New Jersey, and go home. I knew that if I walked into that restaurant and told Henry my truth, I could not take it back. But I did not turn back. I kept going.

I entered the restaurant, where he was waiting for me in a plush, red-velvet booth. He looked well, handsome and comfortable in his skin. Just seeing him gave me the additional courage I needed. He had been brave enough to face the truth of his sexuality and change his life. If he could do it, I could, too. I took a deep breath and slid into the booth.

"Henry," I said, after the preliminary chitchat. "I'm no different than you are. I'm gay. For my whole life, I have locked my gay thoughts in a box in the back of my mind and thought I had thrown away the key. But it's not working. I can't keep everything locked up anymore. I've been torturing myself. I'm going to have to be honest with Jodi, because I'm finally facing the truth myself."

To my amazement, Henry sat back and laughed. "Well, what do you know? One more for the team," he said with a broad smile.

Life Goes On...Thankfully

"Look," he said. "I'm not going to lie to you. It's not going to be a walk in the park. I always knew I was gay. But hiding the way I did with Margie was brutal. I was brutal. I was completely miserable. Margie and I are friends now. We get along better than we ever did while we were married. Our kids have gotten used to the divorce, and we still see each other, and we get along well. They know I'm there for them. They were not happy to face the truth about their father being gay, but we are working it out, conversation by conversation and weekend by weekend. For them, it's so much better than living in a home with parents at each other's throats. It's all going to be okay, Richard, I promise you."

So, that was it. Getting the words out was easy. That was my experience. It was easy. Because I was ready. And, of course, I knew that Henry had survived—even blossomed—in the same situation. He was not a character in a book or a faceless story online, but a man not so different from myself who had faced his truth and changed his life.

Why did it take me so long? This is what I finally understood. You cannot ask a person if he is gay just because you think he is gay. If anyone had asked me, I never would have said I was gay. People come out when they are ready. That was my moment. I was forty-two. That was when I had to come out. I could no longer bear the shame of lying, the shame of pretending to be someone I wasn't, and the exhausting self-hatred involved in being closeted.

~

Of course, that was just the beginning. The euphoria was short-lived. I always thought my sexuality was my own burden to carry. Now Jodi, and so many others whom I loved and cared about, were going to have to deal with it, too.

I was finally ready to face my wife.

"Jodi, can we please have a talk?"

Michael and Rachel were doing their homework upstairs, and I knew we had some time before they emerged. We went to our den, where we had made so many optimistic plans before—how to raise our children, how to expand our roles in the synagogue, how to help those we knew who were in trouble, where to travel, what shows to see. The den was the setting of endless planning to make our happy lives together meaningful and fulfilled. I sat at the desk, and she sat on the sofa.

Since the day I told her I might not stay married to her, she had lost weight, and her easy laugh had vanished. She was very quiet and looked stressed and unhappy. Facing me, she listened to my carefully rehearsed words.

"Jodi, I told you my problem has nothing to do with you. That was the truth. You are not at fault here." I breathed, gathering my strength. I knew I was about to hurl a cannonball at her. "I'm gay, Jodi. I've always suppressed it. I didn't think it would ever affect our marriage. I thought I'd locked it away forever, but I hadn't. It's as if I'm boiling and about to explode. I've been struggling very badly for a long time, but I've finally been able to face it." I pressed on, refusing to stop. "I can no longer stay in the marriage."

It was out. The words were out. I was out. Finally, unbelievably, I had told her.

Inevitably, her eyes welled with tears. She began to bargain. Clearly, she had spoken with her sister, Beth, and they had talked about this possibility, because my words did not shock her as I thought they would.

"I don't care. Stay in the marriage. Just don't get emotionally involved with anyone."

"I can't, Jodi. I can't. It wouldn't be fair to you or to me."

She began to sob. Her perfect life was evaporating. She did not want me to ruin our wonderful life with our children to enter a zone in which she was not prepared to do battle. It was amazing that I did not cry with her. But even as I watched the tears spill from her eyes, heard her words, and sat across from this woman with whom I shared so much, I knew that my decision was right.

"How do you know you really are gay?" she asked.

"I've suppressed it all my life. I thought I had locked it away forever. I thought it was my burden to carry. If there were a magic pill to make these feelings go away, I would definitely take it. I hate the thought that my acceptance of my sexuality would affect the lives of so many other innocent people. I really thought it was just a small part of my personality."

I wished I could tell her the weird mantra I had when we got engaged: I loved her, but I was not perfect. I was nearsighted, right-handed, and felt an attraction to men that I believed would not affect the health of our marriage. But I was twenty-five when we got married, and I couldn't even admit to myself that I was gay.

She pressed me further. "Have you had an affair? Have you met someone else? A man?"

I refused to answer questions about any intimate relationships during our marriage or my current obsession with Gary. I thought it would only hurt her more deeply. Besides, I was deeply ashamed. I could not help myself any longer. She looked stricken. Her normally broad, straight shoulders curved downward as if she carried a boulder on her back.

There was surprisingly little to say. Our conversation ended with me giving her a hug, as if we were old friends parting after a visit. I felt the newborn chasm with relief.

"I love you, Jodi," I said. "I just can't be married anymore." The words were out of my mouth before I could stop myself. I was so grateful that she didn't take out a knife and try to stab me, or worse, scream at me and threaten that I'd never see our kids again.

For the first time in our seventeen years of marriage, I went downstairs to sleep on the couch in the basement.

Jodi began what can only be described as a period of mourning. She spent most of her time on the phone with her sister and attending to our kids. She began to withdraw from friends, unable to share the sorrow she was facing.

I, on the other hand, felt as if I were gathering strength. I was infatuated with Gary, even though we still had not met. Our continuing emails were fortifying. They gave me the strength I needed to hold fast to my decision, lightening my dark thoughts when I wondered what would become of us all. Did we have enough money to live separate lives? Would I still have keys to the house? Would I be a father who picked up his kids by honking in the driveway? Would I only see my children in diners and malls?

I was determined to be decent and aboveboard with my wife. I trusted her and wanted to protect her even while I was breaking her heart. I still wanted to protect my children, who had absolutely no idea what was about to happen to our lives.

Just days later, Jodi and I went to see the premiere of *Hairspray*. I thought about cancelling, because I feared it might upset Jodi with its ribald presentation of a changing world just when ours was falling apart. But selfishly, I decided it would be a terrific show, and she could handle it. Of course, I loved it.

The musical was set in racially charged Baltimore, Maryland, in the 1960s. The score was upbeat, and the story was campy and optimistic, celebrating changes soon to come. White women could fall in love with black men. Fat girls could fall in love with slim, handsome leading men who loved them back. A woman was played by a man. Good could triumph over evil.

Once again, I found solace in the darkened theater and renewed the inner strength to follow my heart. In the car on the way home, though, Jodi, began to cry silently, her faced turned away from me.

"What is it, Jodi?" I asked. Even though I did not want to suppress my growing spirit of independence and I felt buoyed by the show we had just seen, I felt responsibility and guilt for her sorrow.

"Nothing about today. It's just that everything is making me so sad."

I knew *Hairspray* had hit her hard, even though she denied it. I also realized that I had been cruel to take her.

I wanted to rush her, to make her see that I wasn't the only one who would experience the freedom of change despite the upheaval others had to suffer. Jodi would be a participant in a brave new world, whether she wanted to be or not. There was too much at stake for her to pretend, but that was her first instinct.

"I don't want you to move out," she said. "I want you to stay in the marriage. You can do what you want. I don't care." She could not let go. Reflexively, she clung to what she had always known, the life we had created, no matter how altered the current scenario. Who could blame her?

"Just don't leave," she said. "Just don't leave." She kept repeating it over and over.

"I can't stay, Jodi. It wouldn't be fair to you, and it wouldn't be fair to me. I've tried for the last two years to keep this at bay. My coming out is new to you, but it's not to me. I can't get into bed with you every night if you and the marriage no longer have my heart. I know there are other men who would keep their marriages going with their wives complicit, but I can't do that. I've kept the secret for this long, but I don't want to keep it any longer. I need to be true to myself for the first time in my life."

Although I had not planned to say the words that came next, I sensed an opening in front of me. She was weakened, she was aware we were moving in a direction she dreaded. I pressed on.

"I'll be leaving soon," I said, and once the words were out, I could not hold back any longer. I astounded myself with my own unplanned words.

"I want a trial separation that will be our secret. I will live apart from you one night a week and maybe one weekend a month."

"What are you saying? How can you say this?" She began sobbing. "How could you do this? Just don't leave; just don't."

I couldn't believe I had uttered the words. But they were out, and I was relieved. I thought this trial separation would prepare Jodi for the future. It would also give me some time to clear my head and to begin living my new life. Our kids would think I was traveling on business or spending time with friends in New York.

There were no blueprints for my life anymore. I had to say the words I said. I was suffocating at home. I had begun my journey. Even though I was terrified, it felt right, and because of that, I had faith that we would all make it through somehow.

Ten

An Email to Gary

Top Ten Reasons Why Your Wife Should Know That Her Husband Is Gay:

10. You have saved every *Playbill* from every Broadway show you ever saw but throw away *Consumer Reports* magazine before you even bring it into the house.

9. You come home from an NSYNC concert with your eleven-year-old daughter and you are wearing the Joey and Lance headband, not your daughter.

8. You tell your wife you have a cold and miss your son's solo in the spring band concert to stay home to watch the season finale of *Will and Grace*.

7. When you are on the computer and your wife is at home, you keep one hand on the *minimize screen* button at all times.

6. On your anniversary, you are more excited about a Banana Republic gift certificate than about your wife's plan to take you to a B and B for the weekend.

5. When you go to a Bar Mitzvah, you are not only the only husband on the dance floor doing the Macarena, but you can do it better than the DJ.

4. When you have your guy friends over for a game of poker, the most macho CD you can find is *The Love Songs of Michael Bolton*.

Life Goes On...Thankfully

3. Your favorite clients are older women who share their confidential life stories with you, and you relish the tales.

2. At the annual Super Bowl party, you are the only husband in the kitchen talking about the Nordstrom's half-yearly sale, and the only time you go into the TV room is to see the halftime show starring Diana Ross.

1. When the decorator comes over to discuss your great room, you are more concerned about the trim for the throw pillow than where the large-screen TV is going.

Those are my thoughts after spending too many hours on the Garden State Parkway driving "homo" from the shore alone.

~

I went to a funeral one day. It was the kind of funeral at which everyone present questioned how something terrible like that could happen. My good friend Murray had died of a brain tumor. He was forty years old. He was one of the kindest, most positive people I knew.

Many of our friends could not even visit him in the hospital before he died, but Jodi and I had not hesitated. We wanted to go, even though we knew it would be terrible.

He was in pain, and he knew he was dying. He was so happy to see us when we walked into his hospital room.

"Hey!" he said, delighted when he recognized us, despite his weakness. "How are you? Sorry about all the wires and bags you have to look at. What's going on? How are your kids?"

"Murray, our kids are fine. You're here in the hospital, so sick; let's talk about you," I replied. "How are you feeling?"

"No. Richard. Let's face it; your life is so much more interesting."

Could he possibly know that I'd come out? I wanted to tell him, but I did not, even though I knew he would literally take that secret to his grave.

I did not share with him the upheaval in our lives, even though it never left my mind for long, because his illness put our impending change in perspective. I knew that no matter what happened to me, I would always be there for my kids and family. I might be gay, but I was not dying.

Clearly, Jodi had the same thing on her mind, but her concept was in direct opposition to mine. As we walked out, she asked, "Does this make you reconsider all the decisions you are making?"

I knew what she was hoping, but I disappointed her.

"It confirms that I have to live my true life, because we just don't know what the future holds. I realized yet again that I'm forty-three years old, and I have lived all my life for a eulogy."

Her face fell and we walked out of the hospital in silence.

Eleven

I Am Finally What I Am

I was single one day a week and one weekend a month. At long last, it was time to meet Gary. In preparation for the day I'd anticipated for so long, I bought him some carefully considered presents. I selected a Penn State University baseball cap (his college alma mater), made him a cassette of my favorite songs, bought him his favorite candy—peanut M&M's—and the CD of *Dreamgirls*, his favorite Broadway show. I set up the evening carefully, hoping to pick spots he would love. We planned to have drinks at a gay bar and then dinner at a restaurant in Greenwich Village. It was the moment I had been fantasizing about after all those weeks online and on the phone.

We arranged to meet under the huge awning at Penn Station. He was coming up on the train from Philadelphia to meet me. I dressed carefully, wearing a red V-neck sweater over a white T-shirt and tight jeans. I thought this outfit might bring me good luck.

I scanned the crowd under the awning from across the street. It was still rush hour, and there were a lot of people moving around. There was one man who was obviously waiting for someone, and my first thought was, "That's not Gary." But I knew immediately that it was.

Gary-in-the-flesh was anything but the fairy tale that existed in my mind. He did not look at all like I thought, at all like I'd fantasized. I was anticipating someone extraordinary looking, an exceptionally handsome leading man, at whom I would take one look and melt with desire. I was hoping for the embodiment of Sean McDermott, the star of *Miss Saigon*, who was so irresistible to me that I stalked him, despite the danger and inappropriateness of what I was doing.

Instead, I saw an ordinary, unremarkable-looking person wearing a battered baseball cap, a standard-issue down jacket, baggy Gap jeans, and Converse sneakers. From his sloped shoulders and rounded torso, it was clear that he did not work out. Most disappointing of all, he was short. Had I never asked him how tall he was? That was my first requirement in every sexual fantasy I had. I craved a tall man.

Instantly, I understood what I had done. I had created a chimera to make it possible for me to leave my family for the great love that was missing in my life. I had literally made him the object of my dreams. I expected some kind of cosmic sexual thrill when I saw him, the living justification for leaving my family.

I was crushed, but I realized I had behaved like an adolescent, building up the thought of a love affair before I even saw or touched the man. In just those few seconds, I understood what he had told me honestly all along. Gary was gay, divorced, and a father, but he had never come out of the closet and he never would. He was a very successful, highly paid executive with no stomach for coming out in the workplace and he was never going to test his relationship with his kids by asking them to accept his homosexuality.

Any relationship with him would be a deep secret, and I was done with secrets. I knew he would be a great friend, but not a lover.

I approached him, and his face relaxed into a huge, sweet smile. "Who knew you were so handsome?" he said to me.

I gave him all the gifts I brought despite the fact that the Cinderella spell was broken. He took the Penn State baseball hat, the *Dreamgirls* CD, the M&M's, and the cassette of my favorite songs and was overwhelmed. He was not the idyll I had imagined. He was not going to be my next lover and life partner. I was not going to go from Jodi to Gary in a seamless transition. I had to recognize that obsession for the fantasy it was.

But, over drinks and dinner, I appreciated that he was the funny, smart, experienced, and intuitive person I had confided in repeatedly over the internet. I knew he would be my first great gay friend, and he would be an integral part of my new life.

Although restrained by my agreement with Jodi that I would be out only one night a week and one weekend a month, I began to live my gay life in the open in the relative anonymity of New York. I found a small apartment on the West Side in Manhattan, situated so that I could get back to New Jersey and the kids as quickly as possible but private enough for me to start the life I craved. Not for the first time, I drew comfort from the fact that the costume-jewelry business, while not sexy, was lucrative, and I had the financial cushion I needed to set myself up for my new life without threatening the immediate future for Jodi and my children.

~

I had been saving myself for Gary. I wanted my first sexual experience with a man to be with someone I loved, not someone for whom I threw away my "virginity" just to get rid of it. But after meeting Gary, I realized that the perfect man might not be so easy to find.

I could not wait any longer.

I left work, went to my new apartment and showered, and met Henry for a drink. Of course, since I never drink, he asked me what was up.

"I'm going to pick up a guy tonight," I told him. "I'm getting my courage up."

He laughed. "You're kinda pathetic, you know?"

"Yeah, yeah, and you're perfect, right, Henry?"

"Wow," he said. "You really are nervous. This is the conversation of a twelve-year-old."

We laughed, but I was mad at myself for confiding in him. I made an excuse to leave early. "Let me get going. I'm not inviting you along, because you are definitely going to cramp my style. I need a barroom full of strangers."

With that, I left and grabbed a cab and went to The Lion King, an upscale gay bar in Tribeca.

I walked in and stood there for a little while, looking around, feeling both excited and awkward. The place was flashy, with a lot of dark-blue lighting, and a long, sinuous bar that was filled with men, some really handsome, and others not so. Feeling like a character in a movie, I went to the bar, ordered a gin and tonic, and looked around. It didn't take too long. A handsome thirtysomething approached me. I was glad I looked younger than I was.

He really said, "You must be new here...I've never seen you before."

I laughed. He was not gorgeous, but he was good-looking enough, with blond hair, a straight nose, full lips, and good teeth. There was a certain fragility to him that was appealing. He also had a slender but well-built chest, and most appealing of all, he was at least six foot two.

"Would you like to buy me a drink?" he asked.

I took a breath. "Sure."

He ordered a shot of tequila. "Do you like to dance?"

I was at my most agreeable. "Sure."

He leaned in closer to me and said, "After we have some drinks, we could go to a club and go dancing, if you like."

I was nervous and having a hard time making conversation, but he seemed okay and kind of sweet. "Sure," I said again.

As soon as his drink came, he drank it down and ordered another shot. After he downed the second one, he said, "You know, it's so hot in here...Why don't we go outside?"

Life Goes On...Thankfully

I decided to go along. Once we were on the sidewalk in front of the bar, he leaned toward me and kissed me on the mouth and said, "You are really cute. Why don't we skip the club and go straight to a hotel? There's one near here, and it's not too expensive. I go there all the time when I meet guys."

I said, "No problem," even though I was a little worried. Actually, I thought I might be out of my mind, but I decided to keep going. Didn't men get picked up in bars all the time? Most of them didn't get killed or beaten up. I decided to trust my judgment that the guy was handsome, sweet, and not a perverted killer. Plus, I had no interest in a quickie in the toilet stalls.

"Where is it?" I asked, hoping I'd make it out alive, yet determined to continue.

"Just around the corner from here," he said. "I like it there, and it's one of the reasons I come to this bar."

We walked over, and he held my hand. He reached over and put his arm around me, and said, "You really are handsome. I'm so glad you want to play with me."

Well, I guess I did. We got to the hotel, which was kind of tacky but could have been a lot worse, and I paid the person at the desk one hundred dollars in cash.

Up we went to a small, relatively clean room, and he said, "How do you like it? Rough or sweet?"

I said, "Sweet." Then he asked, "Top or bottom?"

I said, "Top."

"Lovely," he answered, and he wriggled out of his pants and pulled me on top of him in an instant. I took the condom out of my pocket and put it on.

"You're so gorgeous," he said. "Don't be nervous..."

"Let's take it slow," I said, laughing a bit with excitement and discomfort. "I don't want to rush."

"No problem, honey," he answered. "I've got all night."

And that is exactly how long we stayed.

He was a bit sophomoric, but I didn't care. He was gorgeous, and he could have sex over and over again. I surprised myself with my own enormous desire. I was overjoyed, even though I knew I wouldn't see him again. I didn't care. I just fucked and fucked; and to me, it was almost devoid of emotional connection, just a physical feeling akin to eating when you've been starving or drinking when you have been dehydrated.

Finally, sated, I told him I had to go, but that I would never, never forget him.

He laughed. "I knew you were sweet."

"Let's go," I said, suddenly overwhelmed by the enormity of what had occurred. "You've exhausted me. It's been a pleasure."

"The pleasure was mine," he purred. "Maybe I'll see you at the bar again!"

Twelve

Breaking News

I told my parents my news in their pretty home in the hills of Litchfield County, Connecticut. I geared up for my announcement by practicing my speech in the car, much as I had done before telling my wife.

I drove up on a glorious fall weekend when the foliage was in full color, but I was so intent on my upcoming news flash that I hardly noticed the blaze of color around me. In the middle of my reverie, I heard the high-pitched *blip blip blip* of a police siren. When I looked in the rearview mirror, sure enough, I saw red and blue lights flashing, and there was a policeman on my tail. He got on his radio and commanded, "PULL OVER."

I checked him out. He was a large man with a big Texas-style hat and a gun in his holster. He didn't look particularly receptive to either a gay flirtation or a self-debasing apology. I tried, nevertheless. "Can you please just give me a warning, officer?" I begged. "I know I was speeding. You can check my record. You'll see I don't have any speeding tickets." I had to laugh at myself. What was I going to tell him? That I was on my way to tell my parents that I was gay, and I was distracted because I thought they'd never love me the same way again or that I would harm our relationship irreparably?

No luck. I got a speeding ticket. I considered it a bad omen.

But, undeterred, I knew I was going to say my piece and hope for the best.

When I got to the house, my parents greeted me warmly. We sat on the screen porch, having coffee, surrounded by trees ablaze in color. My parents knew something was up, because a drive to Litchfield County without some stated purpose was unusual. They had no idea what I was going to say, but they sat patiently waiting for me to get around to the reason for my visit.

I took a breath and began my speech, much as I had with my wife. "I know you are wondering why I'm here. I have to tell you something. I've been wrestling with something for the past two years, and I've realized that I'm gay."

They both sat there silently, my father slightly ashen and my mother looking at me with worry and concern. "I've already told Jodi, and I'm going to do everything I can to avoid hurting her any more. The kids don't know, but I wanted to tell you as well. I'm going to move out of the house for a part of each month, while we figure out the best way to handle this situation. But I don't think we can stay married anymore. I don't want to live a lie."

I admitted I had been in contact with other married gay men, and I knew their compromised lives were miserable.

My mother spoke first and without hesitation. "You have always been a wonderful son, and you are still my son. This does not change anything."

She turned to my father. "Arnold, tell Richard that he has your full support."

"You do," said my father. His face was stern, and his voice full of controlled emotion. "But I think you should see a doctor. And I can't believe you would even think of telling anybody else before you take care of the legal aspects involved here. Your kids might hear something. Call an attorney, and for God's sake find out what you need to know to protect yourself."

It was the best he could do, but it was good enough for me. Call a doctor? For what? To make sure I wasn't having a temporary bout of insanity? To make sure I didn't have AIDS? I decided the attorney part made more sense. I did need to understand what I was going to do to protect us all in the uncharted waters of our future.

But I had gotten what I came for. My mother would never reject me; and my father did not like it, but he would accept my news as well. We were a family, and we would stay a family despite my explosive announcement. Maybe I didn't really surprise them. Perhaps they had a suspicion all along that they never dwelled on or dealt with. They never said. My mother did ask, "How is Jodi taking this?" She had always loved Jodi, and she would never turn her back on her daughter-in-law.

"She's still absorbing the news. It's awful, but I think she is so strong; and day by day, we are working it through. We have no choice."

When I was leaving the house, my mother said to my father, "Arnold, tell Richard you love him."

And he did. Dutifully, but with his voice catching, he said, "I love you, Richard."

Had they both suspected something about me? Once again I wondered, but they never said anything about it, and I never asked. When I hugged my mother, she whispered in my ear, "You know, Richard, it's a good time to be gay." I wasn't sure what that meant, but I thought it meant she would support me in my struggle to live the life I wanted, and she was glad I could do it without the kind of mortal shame that gay men have had to endure historically. Not to mention that AIDS had already crescendoed, and medicines had been found to help to control the virus.

Once I'd told my parents, I told my brothers. I went to lunch with my brother Ronnie at a Chinese restaurant. I told him I was gay.

He was in the middle of eating an egg roll. "Please pass the soy sauce," he said.

"That's it?" I asked, and as befitted the man of few words that he was, he said, "Yup." And that was that.

When I told my brother Robert I was gay, he jokingly said, "I guess you'll need a queen bed from now on." I always thought he was homophobic, but this was not too terrible a reaction.

And my brother Randy said, "So what else is new? I heard a joke today. 'How in hell do you get Dick from Richard? You ask him nicely.'"

It was astonishing to me. My brothers, whom I was close to and yet distant from, all acted completely underwhelmed. There would be no intimate moments when they said they always knew or were disappointed or ashamed or were glad to see me face my fears and come out. I realized again that this was my decision, my life. My brothers were going to live with the truth of my new gay life no differently than they had lived before. These confessions, so difficult to conceive and actually voice, turned out to be little more than nonevents that loomed larger in my brain than in my reality. I was not going to be shunned, avoided, or hated. I was not going to be loved more or less for my suffering.

That was my coming out to my family. They accepted my news with astounding equanimity, if not downright nonchalance. Did they talk about me privately? I was sure they did. But not one of them seemed to want to bring up the subject again, so I decided to leave it be. I couldn't face talking about it, and no one seemed to be eager to beat the new drum. So I took the easy way out and decided to let the news settle in for a while.

Jodi wanted to postpone the inevitable for as long as possible; *never*, being her preference. Our children still had no idea what was going on. We decided that we would live together as a family with no public announcements but with the ongoing trial separation until just after Rachel's big day, her Bat Mitzvah.

Thirteen

Rachel's Bat Mitzvah

In October 2002, I went to London on my first business trip as an emotionally separated man. I went to see a one-woman show starring the American comedienne Elaine Stritch called *Elaine Stritch at Liberty*. She was a legendary gay icon like Judy Garland, and I was happy to see the show since I'd missed the New York engagement. I did not know much about her life, but I knew she had lived a hard life when she uttered the lyric, "Good times and bad times, I'm still here."

I sat in the theater mesmerized by her tales of seesaw finances, alcoholism and stardom, failures and successes. At the close of the show, Ms. Stritch came back to sing her encore, "I Must Have Done Something Good," from *The Sound of Music*. I sat in the theater and cried, because I felt that could be my anthem, as well.

The Sound of Music is one of my favorite musicals. Maria and the captain find love and live happily ever after, despite the terrible war that rages around them, his ridiculous whistle and crusty personality, and her immature, undisciplined ways. The captain is so terrified of love that he abandons his children, and Maria avoids love by cloistering herself in an abbey. But Mother Superior tells Maria, "You have to face your fear." As soon as they open themselves to love, they must risk their lives to stand by their principles. They have to climb over the Swiss Alps with seven children to get to safety, and they accomplish it.

The next day, I wrote my first fan letter ever. It was to Ms. Stritch, telling her about coming to terms with my sexuality and how her show touched me so. Four days later in New York, I received a letter from her.

Dear Richard,
Thank you for your dear, sweet letter. Shakespeare said, "to thine own self be true." Best of everything. Stand tall.
Love, Elaine.

That letter was the first framed piece to hang on the wall of my new apartment in New York.

Four months later, Jodi and I threw the party to end all parties for our daughter, Rachel. When Jewish children reach the age of thirteen, they are considered to be adults who accept responsibility for their own Jewish lives. For the first time, they may read from the Torah, the ancient book of Jewish laws and history. They prepare for months for the ceremony, and they usually read in Hebrew before a congregation full of friends and family. It is a milestone in Jewish life for observant Jewish families.

In the suburban world of privilege in which we lived, the important religious part was all too often overshadowed by the over-the-top parties that followed when the grueling synagogue service was complete.

Jodi and I tried to keep the solemnity and ceremony of the occasion paramount, but we were not beyond wanting a big and happy party to celebrate the moment, either.

We'd celebrated Michael's Bar Mitzvah two years earlier. It was filled with ceremony and the love of family and friends. Since I was the temple president at the time, it felt especially joyful. We wanted nothing less for Rachel, even though, unbeknown to her, our marriage was breaking apart.

Jodi did not want Rachel's Bat Mitzvah to be ruined by our impending separation. She was still hoping against hope that we would not separate, and even though I knew that hope was futile, I agreed to wait until after the Bat Mitzvah. I couldn't figure out a

Life Goes On...Thankfully

better way. I had waited as long as I could, and despite the dramatic timing, that was the plan.

Rachel was looking forward to her big day, studying three times a week at synagogue. She was excited to have all the family and friends at her big party.

On the day of Rachel's Bat Mitzvah, only seventeen of the 205 people present knew that our marriage was ending and that we would shortly announce our separation. Even the rabbi was unaware, because I feared he would change the personal blessing he bestowed upon Rachel and the sermon for the day if he knew the real drama that was about to unfold.

The planning for the party was meticulous. We gathered photos of the family on vacations through the years and shots of all of our many friends. The photos were shown on a video screen all night long. Jodi and I offered up additional welcome speeches. We had a meal fit for a king—kosher, of course—and party favors and music and dancing. Impossible as it sounds, I tried to keep all the hoopla for the party slightly subdued, aware of the irony of what was to follow—the bizarre announcement that our family was breaking up.

Jodi and I had only one fight before the Bat Mitzvah. We had the option of entering the party room as a family, holding hands, in a theatrical spotlight and under a giant arch made of big, multicolored balloons. I said no, and justified my refusal saying the balloon arch was too expensive. I really thought it was just too abrasive an image. Our whole family under a rainbow? The rainbow was also a gay symbol, which was ironic at best and tasteless at worst—even though it was actually my dream that our family would somehow remain miraculously united.

Uncharacteristically, Jodi suddenly dug her heels in. "I want the rainbow," she insisted. "I don't care how much it costs."

And so, of course, I gave in, guilt ridden and dreading the fallout ahead.

~

Rachel's big day started at Dunkin' Donuts with our traditional pink doughnuts and chocolate milk. Next, I took her to a salon to get her hair done. I was glad to get out of the house, because Jodi and I were both nervous. Our conversations were stilted and polite, and we had Jodi's sister and her family staying with us for the weekend, heightening the bizarreness of our deception.

Rachel was excited and nervous, oblivious to our hidden concerns. She chattered away. "Dad, what if I botch my haftorah? What if I forget everything I studied? What if I trip and fall while going up to the bimah?"

We laughed. She had been studying for months. She had practiced in front of Jodi and me many times. We knew she had her prayers down cold. I loved her more than ever, my heart aching. I knew that she could not even imagine what was about to befall her.

When we arrived at the synagogue, the parking lot was already beginning to fill with family and friends. Rachel was glittering in pink and purple, her favorite colors since babyhood. Michael was dressed in a navy-blue suit, looking every bit the lanky, cool older brother, glad his own Bar Mitzvah was well past, and he did not have to say the difficult prayers. Jodi was resplendent in a red satin suit. She hardly spoke to me but kept up a prattle with Michael and Rachel.

The service went according to tradition, Hebrew prayers read and songs sung. Rachel read her Torah portion without one mistake, reciting the ancient prayers exactly as she had in our many moments of preparation. I marveled at her composure, so grateful that at thirteen, she seemed so strong. Jodi teared up while we each gave a personal blessing to Rachel in front of the ark where the Torah was stored.

Jodi's words to Rachel were filled with portent. "You are one of the most loving, warm, and understanding people I know. You are also strong, resourceful, and generous in both your words and your actions." She went on, but I could barely listen, so strongly

Life Goes On...Thankfully

did I feel the weight of my own intentions and the hope that my children would be resilient.

"Rachel," I said, holding her hands in mine. "There can be no doubt of our love for you and our delight in your sweet and generous character. We know that you are growing into a woman who will cherish the values you have been taught at home and here in this synagogue..."

I could not escape the image of a split screen in my mind. I pictured myself uttering my loving words, but I also pictured myself as a fraud, a Judas, a master of betrayal. I knew that very shortly, I would be splitting up this family I had nurtured like a bird building a nest, straw by straw; protecting the eggs; and finally putting the worms in the mouths of our chicks' eager beaks. Now, when they would have to leave the nest, did they know how to fly? Would I destroy them for my own personal needs? And what of my friends and family, all present for this life event?

I knew that many would be shocked, disappointed, and confused. How could this perfect family be headed for a breakup? They would all say the same thing. "We just celebrated Rachel's Bat Mitzvah, and now they are separating?"

I also knew many people would figure out the true reason, because what else could come between our fantastic poster-perfect family, which everyone admired?

It was one of the most complex, emotional productions I had ever conceived. No one knew the real ending, especially not my daughter.

Rachel was triumphant, giggling with relief. There was dancing to a very long hora, the traditional Jewish celebratory dance, and a big cake with thirteen candles, each lit in dedication to beloved family members and friends. The band played on, with most guests dancing till the very end. Finally we said good-night to the stragglers, accepted our congratulations, and headed home.

Jodi was exhausted and quiet when we arrived. I knew she was hoping the party would change my mind and that I wouldn't actually go through with my plan, but I gave no indication that I was weakening. I ended the night of my daughter's Bat Mitzvah sleeping on the couch.

Fourteen

Family Meeting

Jodi and I went to a psychologist to get professional help with upending the lives of our children. The psychologist was clear in her directives. "As long as the lives of your kids are not really changing, they will be less afraid, and they will adapt. Don't tell them you are separating because of your sexuality. It's too much of a blow.

"Tell them one thing at a time. First, tell them you are separating because of marital problems, but they can continue to live their lives as they have before—in their home, at their schools, and with their father around almost as much as before. Then, later, let them know about your sexuality. But not at first."

So, that was our script. I planned to follow it to the letter.

I knew I was going to hurt them. But I believed my children would still love me, and that in the end, it would be all right. Even as I mourned for their lost innocence, I hoped their inner strength would prevail.

I craved more than anything in the world to do this right, fix it so it would be okay, so that I could breathe again. There was no going back. I had always believed in the power of happy endings, and I hoped that I was going to have mine.

~

Rachel was thirteen and Michael, fifteen, when they received inconceivable news from the person they thought least likely in the world to betray them.

We sat in our den after I called a family meeting. Rachel looked at me warily, curling a lock of hair around a finger. Michael made no eye contact at all; he just looked down, kicking his feet against the sofa.

I could feel my heart beating, but I forced myself to speak the words I had been practicing silently for weeks. "I have something difficult to tell you. Your mother and I are going to have a trial separation. We've grown apart, even though we still like each other. But we are no longer as much in love as we were before. We're going to try to work it out, but I'm going to get an apartment in New York and sleep there instead of home. Your lives will not really change, because I am going to be home for supper almost every night anyway, and I will only go into New York after you go to bed."

Jodi was poised. The only sign that she was nervous was the darting of her eyes back and forth between Rachel and Michael, assessing the damage as the words fell from my lips. She did not cry. She held Rachel's hand while I spoke. Michael looked down, silent.

Jodi, leaning forward toward them, her back straight and stiff, said, "I know this is a shock, and I know it's hard to believe. But we are going to be okay, and we will get through this."

I could never have done it without Jodi's steady, matter-of-fact delivery and her endorsement of this bewildering turn in their lives. She offered optimism even though her own heart was breaking, all for the sake of our children's equanimity.

Neither child said a word. They had no idea how to react. Michael's eyes never once met mine, and Rachel sat quietly, still twisting her hair with her forefinger.

"Do you have anything you want to ask us?" I pressed. But they had no questions, and their silence made the announcement an underwhelming moment after the weighty and daily anxiety I had been experiencing.

We released them. It took all of fifteen minutes. They practically ran out of the room.

The day after we told the children we were separating, Jodi called her mother to tell her the news. It was all the more difficult because Maxine had recently been diagnosed with breast cancer and was being treated with radiation therapy. The last thing Jodi wanted to do was upset her mother further, but she had no choice. Maxine was now alone. Jodi's father had been her lifelong companion, but he had passed away two years prior from pancreatic cancer.

Jodi told her mother the entire truth: that I was gay, and that this crisis had been going on for months, that we'd waited till after the Bat Mitzvah, and finally told the kids we were separating.

As soon as Jodi hung up with her mother, my office phone rang. It was my mother-in-law. I took the call, praying for absolution.

"Richard," she said, her voice breaking. "I want you to know that I love you and I hope I can always consider you my son. I am not angry with you. I understand. But I expect you to be good to my daughter and make sure you take care of her."

Translation: I would not lose her love, despite what was happening. But she let me know that I was to be held accountable for that love and trust. I had no intention of abandoning my responsibilities, so for me, that call was one more step forward.

I was glad that Jodi's father was not present, though. Lou was the warm, emotive father I never had. I knew Lou loved me, but I wasn't sure that he would have been as gracious or forgiving as Jodi's mother was, and the thought that I'd significantly let him down would have been a difficult sadness to overcome.

Each night, as I promised, I left New York after work and came home for dinner. I helped Jodi clean up after dinner, staying till the children went to bed at ten o'clock and then drove back to my new apartment in Manhattan. We began a new kind of relationship that even Jodi and I could not find the words for.

Sometimes our nightly contact was too much for her, and she could not be in the same room with me. She went out with her friends just to get away from me. Sometimes evening activities for school and friends meant we had driving obligations, which were always a big relief. We settled into a new, bizarre pattern, but there were no crises, and I began to believe the therapist was right. The routines were not upended, and Jodi's willingness to do what was necessary to protect her children made my small sacrifice to travel to New Jersey each weeknight pale in comparison.

I promised myself that I would always take care of Jodi. We both had divorce attorneys, and we both told our attorneys that we were not the usual, acrimonious couple. I wanted Jodi to be treated with respect and generosity, and that is exactly what happened. I never regretted that decision. It was one of the bedrocks of our ongoing relationship.

Six months later, we told our children we were definitely getting a divorce, but we still did not tell them I was gay. We were back in the den again, taking our usual places in what was once the best room in the house. Jodi sat with squared shoulders on the edge of the sofa, holding back her ever-ready tears.

I took a deep breath and began. "Our separation has clarified for both of us that we are getting a divorce after all, but we are still a family, even though things are changing. We both still love you, and your lives won't change a whole lot. We will still be right here in this house; I will still be here a lot, and we will do everything we can to make sure you are okay."

Forcing herself to be complicit, but still maintaining her fierce determination that our children feel protected, Jodi said, "Dad is right. We will still be a family, although it might not feel exactly like it once did. But never doubt our love for you both."

Life Goes On...Thankfully

There was a long, uncomfortable silence. Michael refused to look at either one of us and said nothing. Finally, he looked at his watch. "I don't want to miss the opening kickoff of the Jets game."

Jodi pressed Rachel for a reaction, and she said, "Please stop asking me how I'm doing. I'm doing fine."

Jodi said, "I know this is a sad situation, and that you each wish it was different."

Rachel, eyes downcast, said softly, "There's nothing I can do about it."

Michael shrugged.

And we released them.

We comforted ourselves with the thought that they were not showing signs of trouble. Their grades were good, they were eating well and sleeping through the night, they had plenty of friends, and happily, they had no alopecia, bulimia, or drug habits.

Would I still take a magic pill to be straight? No, honestly, I wouldn't. I did wish my decision affected only me, but I had no regrets about my life with Jodi. I loved that life and all the richness it brought me. But I was undeniably happy to be living the next chapter of my life. This was my new journey. I embraced it. It was right for me, even though I was scared of what was to come.

~

There was a snowstorm the day I told my children I was gay. It was six months to the day since I had moved out, a date I circled on my calendar, following the therapist's advice to move slowly but steadily toward telling my children the truth about my sexuality.

I was not home when they woke up that morning. I was in New York, carrying out my plan to be home each evening for dinner but departing for the city after they went to bed. I pictured them shrieking with joy when they awoke to see the snowflakes falling so thickly on our beautiful lawn and finding out school was cancelled for the day.

They spent the day sledding with friends, baking brownies with Jodi, and watching television, unexpectedly freed from their routine.

All day, I mentally rehearsed the speech I would give to them that night. I wrote it down to memorize it. I was sure of my direction, but not at all certain of the outcome. Gary called to wish me luck. He meant it. I knew he cared about me and my family. I was about to do something he could never have envisioned doing himself.

I thought about my own father, who, while protective and responsible, had held back the warmth of his love for me. I was often the favorite of many adults in my life, but I had been unsuccessful in creating a bond with my father. There was a barrier I could never cross, a barrier with no words or distinct outlines, but it existed, nonetheless. I had worked my whole married life to offer my unconditional love to my children, a love they could take for granted, certain I'd be there always. I knew they had no preparation for what lay ahead. Despite the bomb I was about to drop, I was still the father they knew and loved, but I was a sexual human being, and I was asking them to understand that.

That night, we sat down at the kitchen table for one of our favorite meals, meatballs and spaghetti, which Jodi had prepared. We had no trouble finding subjects to talk about—the snow, of course, and school, vacations, sports, and their hope that they might get one more snow day the next day. Jodi was a bit subdued, plagued by her own fears.

I was surprised I could eat, with all the emotion I was bottling up inside. I could feel the five pages of notes I had written to myself pressing against my body in my back pocket.

After dinner, we all cleaned up. I kept wondering, was this the Last Supper?

Just as the kids started to head upstairs, I said, "Hang on, guys. Your mother and I want to talk to you."

Life Goes On...Thankfully

Jodi wanted to tell them separately, but I thought we should be a family unit. I wanted them to hear identical words, and selfishly, I was not sure I could get the *g* word out twice. I told them we would speak to them in the den, wondering if they would ever watch TV in there again after this conversation.

My children had a way of waiting, eyes open, heads turned toward me. They could be optimistic, hoping we would introduce a new vacation or a newly pregnant family member; or just impatient, waiting to get to the television for the evening. Surely they were on inner alert, scorched from two previous meetings when we told them we were separating and then divorcing.

I took a deep breath and began. "This is not a joke. I want you to know the real reason that Mom and I are getting divorced." I swallowed and forced myself to go on. "I've struggled with my own sexuality for a long time, and I now realize that I am gay."

I could not believe I could get that word out of my mouth. It was the hardest thing I ever had to say.

"Mom has known for over a year. She is okay with it. Your grandparents and aunts and uncles know, too, and everyone is supportive and accepting."

They just sat there. Michael was expressionless, and Rachel was looking at me, listening intently. I forced myself to continue. "I think you are old enough to hear the truth, and perhaps this will make the upcoming divorce less confusing. Most important of all, Mom and I have had a good marriage. We did not fight, and we've had many wonderful times, but because I'm gay, we can't be married anymore."

Jodi stepped in. "It hasn't been easy for me, but Dad has been honest and struggled with this realization. I've known for a while what the situation really is, and we've talked and talked about the best way to handle it all. He has to be true to who he is, and I know he will always love us all, even if he is not going to live here. We can't be married anymore because he is gay, and even though it's hard for me, I accept it."

She teared up and kept going. "He will still be your father, and he will remain in our lives. That will never change."

How she did it, I'll never know. I did know that without her, I would have lost them.

"You should know a few things," I said. "I'm happy being gay. It's normal, but maybe not common to be gay, and is not a disease or an illness. I'm still your dad. I'm still the person you love. I don't look or act differently than I did a year ago. I'm not going to wear dresses or earrings. I still love you, and we will still be a family."

The talk took twenty minutes.

Jodi asked, "Do you have any questions?"

They both said no. Rachel asked if she could go upstairs to do her homework.

I just couldn't let Michael retreat silently. It was too important a moment, so I fell back on the way we usually connected, knowing a verbal interaction would be too big a struggle for him. "Michael," I said, "do you want to play Ping-Pong?"

He agreed. We went to the basement and hit the ball back and forth, back and forth, playing exactly the way we always did, perhaps somewhat mechanically, but the movement was a relief to me. He didn't look me in the eye, and I didn't let him win. He didn't try to smash the ball in my face, and I didn't try to make him talk. We played our usual game, and we lost ourselves in it, to my utter amazement.

When we trooped back upstairs, as we had so many times before, I felt a bit better. I hoped he understood my subliminal message—that although I had dropped a bomb on him, I was still the father he loved, even if he hated my news.

Jodi was with Rachel, who was crying.

Jodi spoke for her. "Rachel doesn't understand how you could be married to me and now be gay. She's also worried about being embarrassed in the community."

I was grateful to get an initial concern that I could try to alleviate. I was ready with the answer. "Rachel, when I married your mother, I really didn't know I was gay. It was a realization that came to me over many, many years. As far as your embarrassment about who knows and who doesn't, I can tell you that some of our friends already know because I've told them, and I am going to tell the rest, one by one, so you don't have to."

This seemed to comfort her, and when it was time for bed, I sat at her bedside and said, "Rachel, there are no more family powwows. You know everything. There are no more surprises around the corner."

When I went back to New York that night, I told myself yet again that I owed it all to Jodi. Without her, I could have lost my children. Because of her, I had hope that my children would continue to love me.

It was January 15, 2004. I was forty-four years old. I was finally free to be my true self.

Fifteen

Making the Rounds

I began to tell our closest friends that I was gay. At times, I felt like an author on a book tour. Same story, different store. It was both authentic and automated. Our best and most loyal friends in New Jersey. My closest friends from college. First the rings of our friendships that were very close, and next the ones that were more peripheral. I wanted people to hear from me that I had changed. I did not want to be the object of gossip, and of course, I wanted to protect Jodi, Michael, and Rachel as much as I could. I knew I had to make it personal and honest.

I started with our best friends and neighbors, Michael and Heidi. I called in advance and told them I had something important to share. We greeted each other at the door with our usual embraces and jokes, but they knew something was different, because Jodi wasn't with me. When I was seated in their living room, I looked around, took a deep breath, and got to the point.

"I've got some personal news, and I'm a little nervous," I began. I could feel the sweat trickling down the back of my neck.

Michael laughed. "You, nervous? Since when are you nervous? What's up?" Could my friend have read my mind?

Heidi just sat there, perched on her sofa, waiting. Our kids had spent countless hours together and had innumerable sleepovers, and we had taken many vacations together. Could they possibly suspect what I was going to say? I had no idea, but I plunged ahead.

"Over these last many months, I have realized my true sexuality. It's been both a brutal and a life-altering experience, but I've understood that I'm gay. I had some inklings during my life, but I always ignored them and pushed those thoughts and feelings to the back burner of my mind. But over the past months, I found that I could no longer do it. I couldn't hide it from myself, and I couldn't hide it from Jodi. The last thing I wanted to do was hurt or disappoint her, and I knew that if I began to live with deceit and lies, I'd hate myself and shame my family. I decided to come out, be honest, and try to make it somehow come out okay. I can't live a lie, and ultimately I believe that the people who love me will eventually understand and not abandon me. And that's what I came to tell you.

"Jodi, Michael, and Rachel know. It's been a long, slow, and deliberate process. Now I'm telling our friends, hoping that my family will not be punished for my decision to come out.

Jodi and I are getting a divorce, but we are still the parents of two people we love most in the world, and we don't want to hurt them. We've decided we are going to forge ahead with our heads up high. I'll continue to be part of their lives in Wyckoff, even though I'll be living in an apartment in New York, and I'd like to remain in our synagogue, where I feel like such an integral part. But I don't want to and cannot live a lie."

Michael and Heidi sat and listened without interruption. Their faces did not reveal anything about what they were thinking.

Heidi spoke first. "Richard, we love you. We love Jodi and Rachel and Michael, and we would never, ever turn our backs on you or them. We respect you, and we will help you any way we can."

Michael said, "You are going to shock a lot of people, Richard, but most of the people we know love you. The rest are jealous of you. Try not to worry so much. It's huge, I know, but you are all going to be okay. Times are changing, Richard. It's a shock to come out, but thank God we don't live in a conservative place where you'd be run out of town and your wife and children humiliated."

"How is Jodi handling this?" Heidi asked. I could see her concern for her dear friend whose life was obviously imploding.

"Jodi is the strongest person I know," I said. "She has to accept something that is abhorrent to her, a divorce, but she's willing to do it amicably to protect our kids, and she's willing to forgive me for the sake of family. I'm not sure I deserve her. Or ever did."

Heidi rushed to add her support. "We'll be there for her, too. Our friendship will not change. We love you all too much."

Her next words surprised me. "Now, tell us something juicy. Are you dating anyone? Have you fallen in love?"

And that was pretty much how it went. I took this same message to everyone and got the positive feedback I needed to keep going. Only one of my friends said he thought I should have waited till our kids were both out of high school, and that was the one friend I had always suspected was living a double life as a gay man and husband. The rest of my friends stood by me and my family. Whatever might have been said behind my back, I was met with understanding and sympathy everywhere I went.

Sixteen

A Game I Play

Jodi was right. It was much easier to take a business trip than to stay at home with the usual responsibilities. I thought of this as I flew to London on a short trip for work.

When the plane took off, I watched the thick, cushiony clouds passing below me and the serene blue sky above and let myself think about how happy I felt. I expected the trip to go well. I got along brilliantly with the client, a charming older woman who usually bought more than enough costume jewelry to make the expense of the trip well worth it. I felt powerful and optimistic, dizzy with new possibilities. I had been incredibly lucky. My life, though completely upended, did not fall apart. My kids remained loyal and seemingly psychologically intact, and our friends and family didn't reject me. It was almost too good to be true.

After an excellent meeting and a side trip to the Tate Museum, I took the client to see *Joseph and the Amazing Technicolor Dreamcoat* at the West End. I couldn't wait to take Rachel to see it on Broadway. I loved the combination of biblical story and irreverence, Judaism and musical theater, and I sympathized with Joseph, who had so many brothers to deal with. I only had three, and they were enough. But even though they tried to kill him and sold him off as a slave, Jacob was ultimately able to forgive his brothers and enjoy being a family again.

Like Jacob, I ended up happy enough with my relationship with my brothers. We were each proud of the growth of our company and our roles in it. And they had made it possible for me to get through the darkest days of my self-discovery. My work had undeniably suffered, yet no one had blamed me for my distraction or ridiculed me for coming out.

Where once I obsessed about the secret opportunities my London trips afforded me—I'd never forgotten the bathhouse—I now looked forward to returning to New York. Several months earlier, a man had entered my life like a blazing rocket. I was totally besotted and in full-throttle lust. He was the best-looking man I ever dated—movie-star handsome with rich-brown hair; a chiseled chin; and a lithe, strong, beautiful body.

~

Robert and I met on the internet during my search for my first great gay love. We exchanged gorgeous, sexy, flirty emails and texts for weeks, and then I went to Washington, DC, for work. That gave me the perfect excuse to meet him in Philadelphia, where he lived.

We met at a restaurant that he selected, a dark, beautifully appointed French bistro with a wood tables and gilt-edged mirrors. I saw him standing at the bar when I entered. From my first glance at his tall, graceful, muscular frame, I was hooked. I could practically hear the sizzle. It was love, lust, and heat and obsession all at one time.

"Wow," I said, walking over as casually as I could. "You certainly make a good first impression. And you haven't opened your mouth yet."

He smiled. "Then I guess I better not talk too much. I'd hate to ruin a good thing."

That weekend, we couldn't leave each other alone. The sex was astonishing, the conversation diverting. I was convinced that all the suffering I had been through to come out and all the pain I had put my family through was behind me. I had discovered an intoxicating new love that made all the upheaval worth it.

But time does tell.

After several smoldering weekends in Philadelphia, where we only got out of bed to eat, he said he wanted to visit me in New York over the New Year's holiday. I couldn't wait to celebrate New Year's Eve with him, show him my world, and take him to my favorite places. Of course, the first thing I did was buy theater tickets. I made a few phone calls and paid way too much for two tickets to *The Boy from Oz* with Hugh Jackman, a very, very hot ticket on Broadway. It was a Peter Allen production and promised to be a gay extravaganza. I wanted him to share my visceral love for the theater, and I felt sure this show would impress him.

The morning he was to come, the phone rang.

"How are you, gorgeous?" I said. "I've got our whole evening planned, but I won't tell you a thing yet."

His tone was flat. "I'm afraid I have some disappointing news, Richard. I'm not going to be able to come to see you in New York. Something ridiculous has come up. You know my roommate who's been in California for so long? He's come back and wants to paint the apartment over the weekend. I've promised to help him, and I can't get out of it. He's been so generous with me, letting me live here and all—I just can't say no."

I fought back my tears. I knew instantly that he was lying, that they were lovers, and that I had just been a pastime until his lover came back. I was jealous and sickened.

"You're painting your apartment over New Year's Eve weekend?" I managed to choke out. "That's the best excuse you could come up with?"

I hung up, completely crushed. Even though I knew I was new to the whole gay life, I already imagined I had found the love of my life, a soul mate with whom I could share physical intimacy and emotional connection. Apparently not. I always thought I was a good judge of character, but he had really deceived me with his ardor and his smoky good looks and witty conversation. I had been blind to any sign that I should take it slowly.

We did not see or speak to each other for three weeks, and then the emails began anew. Somehow, I forgot my hurt as he turned on all the considerable charm he possessed to win me back.

And he succeeded.

"Are you sure you want to do this?" I asked, knowing I certainly did. "I can't share you with another person. I'm not capable of that."

"Richard, I've never met anyone like you. I can't forget you. I think about you all the time. I'm sorry about what I did, but all that is over, I promise. He's moved out. We had a rocky relationship to begin with, and we won't be seeing each other ever again."

I was still hurting enough to be wary. "Are you really in? You have to decide. Drama is fine for Broadway, but lying and cheating make me ill. It's not the way I want to live my life."

"I agree completely. I was awful, and I'm sick over it. I just want to be together again."

And so we were. We had another spectacular weekend, and the relationship began anew. More fabulous sex, more luminous weekends, more walking on air.

~

So, I was daydreaming about returning to Robert as I flew back from London after that business trip. Suddenly, in the middle of the flight, I felt sharp, lightning pains in my chest. At first, I was just stunned. But as the flight went on, the pains grew more searing, and I went over the edge into terrified.

The most obvious explanation was a heart attack, but that thought was so ridiculous that I immediately ruled it out. I was only forty-four. It simply was not in the realm of possibility.

When the pains did not recede, I began to reassess what was possible. I didn't want to spend my last hours on an airplane all by myself without any of my family to say good-bye to, and I certainly did not want the crew fussing over me on the flight. I resisted the impulse to ask for help, determined to get off the plane and find out what was wrong with me when I landed.

I made it out of the airport and into a cab. In the taxi from John F. Kennedy Airport, I called my trusted childhood friend, Sam, who was a cardiologist. Sam practically grew up in my family kitchen with my brothers and me. Just hearing his familiar voice saying hello on the phone reassured me.

"Sam, I can't believe it, but I'm having chest pains. Could I be having a heart attack?"

"Listen carefully, Richard. Do not go home to your apartment. Go to the Emergency Room of the nearest hospital. Now."

"I don't want to be worked on by a stranger. I want you there."

"Richard. Hospital. Now."

"Sam, I've made it from London without keeling over. Now, where can I meet you?"

"Fine. Englewood Hospital. I'll be waiting at the ER door. And, so help me, if you're not dead, I may kill you."

The additional twenty minutes in the cab didn't kill me, and neither did Sam.

The Emergency Room was bedlam. I was the center of attention of a team of technicians and doctors led by Sam, who wired me up to screens and monitors and poked my blood vessels, looking for answers in EKG tapes, blood chemistries, and repeat urine samples, even as they assured me I would be fine. Through the beeps and alarms, the squeak of rubber soles, and the rushing of staff, I heard Sam on the phone with one of my brothers. I could tell by Sam's tone that something was happening, but, with all the commotion around me, I couldn't really decipher what it was.

At one point, Sam told me, "The chest X-ray shows a spot on your lung. We don't have to worry about it because you don't smoke, but we need to check it out further."

I had no idea what he was talking about. What did that have to do with the searing chest pains? I pushed it aside, worrying about the obvious way before the occult.

I was admitted to the Cardiac Care Unit. The tests and monitoring continued, assuring, alarming, and otherworldly, all at once.

I called Jodi to let her know what was happening to me. She came to the hospital immediately. When I saw her familiar presence, I instantly felt better. She was always there for me, and this time was no different. She looked stricken and vulnerable. Her eyes were full of concern, and I felt our deep connection still strong even after all I had put her through.

With her voice quavering, she asked, "Richard, what's happening? Have you had a heart attack? What's wrong with you?"

"It's probably nothing, Jodi. It's scary, but I think it's over now."

"How can you say that? You don't know anything yet." She began crying and apologized for her tears when I was the one who was sick and in pain. "We've gone through so much already, and now this? Michael and Rachel will be so frightened."

She was right. It was frightening, but I tried to minimize the likelihood that I'd had a heart attack with some denial rooted in fact. "There is no history of cardiac disease in the family. Why would I be an outlier?"

She sat with me a while longer, still my wife in name, still in love with me, and still half-hoping that somehow all these terrible events of the past year would evaporate. She had to tear herself away to go home. Once again, I was guilt ridden and ashamed. I had put her through so much, and she was as loyal as ever.

The chest pains had ceased, and the doctors thought it was safe to send me home. They could find nothing in the tests to indicate that I'd had a heart attack.

The next morning, following Sam's instruction, I returned to the hospital to have a PET scan to follow up on that bothersome spot on my lung. PET scans identify and illuminate cancerous tumors with dye. I couldn't eat or drink, and I had to lie on a hard table and be inserted into a gigantic machine, but all in all, it wasn't too bad. After the procedure, a bit shaken but still certain I'd be all right, I went to work.

I was walking toward the corner of Fortieth Street and Broadway in midtown Manhattan to meet a client for lunch when I got a call on my cell phone from Sam.

"You lit up the damned PET scan," Sam said. "Your right lung has cancerous growths in two of the three lobes."

At the moment he said that, I couldn't understand how life-altering those words were. I knew it was bad news, but it really had no real meaning. Or the meaning hadn't sunk in yet.

After a couple of seconds, I said, "So...what happens next?"

"You are going to have to see a cancer specialist, Richard, to figure out what to do."

I barely registered his next reassuring comments and directives, but as soon as we hung up, I canceled my lunch with the client and called my brother Ronnie, who was nearby at our office. He was stunned by the news, but somehow we both knew it wouldn't be real until my parents heard about it. Together, we left New York and drove to our parents' house in Connecticut to tell them the results of the PET scan. I had yet to utter the words *lung cancer*. I simply could not believe it.

~

We drove down the long, quiet country road that led to their house. A recent storm had left a couple of inches of snow on the front lawn. The garage door had been raised for us so we could come in and take our shoes off in the mudroom. When we entered the house, I could see down the hall into the kitchen, where my mother was standing. She was wearing an apron, busy cooking something for the unexpected lunch, happy we were coming to spend time with her and my father. I could see the table, already set for four, with some fresh flowers she had purchased earlier with our gathering in mind. She had absolutely no idea what was going to happen next.

Unfortunately, I did. I knew she would be so happy to see me, and that I was going to ruin her life. I felt her pain first, well before I considered my own.

My mother was no stranger to losing a loved one. A younger brother whom she'd adored had suffered from bipolar disease. During one significant depression, he committed suicide. She spoke of him often, even though it had been many years since he died. Each time she did, I ached for her, for her pain and for the fact that no matter how much she loved all the men in her life, she had never gotten over the loss of her baby brother.

I knew my diagnosis was going to plunge her into the same sort of grief. I chose my words carefully, but there was no way to disguise the weight of my news. They knew I had been checked out in the hospital after having the initial chest pain, but they had been told I was cleared of a heart attack and discharged.

After the greetings and hugs, we sat down for lunch. As soon as they asked me how I was feeling, I took a breath, trying to keep my voice even. "There was another finding during the initial tests. My chest X-ray showed some spots on one of my lungs, so Sam had me in for a PET scan this morning. He said two of the three lobes of the right lung are affected. He said the spots show that I have lung cancer." My words seemed unbelievable, especially to me.

My father sat in quiet shock, his face suddenly gray and grief-stricken, his shoulders sagging with the weight of the news I had just delivered. My mother, however, surprised me. She had no room or time for grief; she paused for a moment as she absorbed the news, her face betraying no weakness or shock. Then she straightened her back and swung into action. She took over as the expert in charge.

"Richard, we are going to get the best medical advice there is. I'm sure you can beat this thing, and we are going to find the best surgeon out there to manage whatever care you need. Do not despair."

My mother long ago had left her job as a decorator and gone to graduate school to become a genetic counselor. We were all immensely proud of her achievement. Because of her work, she had some significant medical contacts, and she called them all. She called in every favor she had, every source she thought would help. She called so many people that the recommendations began to repeat themselves, and that was how she found the best doctors. It was surreal. She directed me, told me exactly what to do, and I did it. I was in shock and denial. She was clear and directed. We went back and forth from New York to Boston, seeking experts' opinions on the best course of action to take.

My friends always teased me about my propensity to plan. I am the guru of long-range planning, the king of advance tickets, the most prepared and the least spontaneous guy you will ever meet. Creating memories for my loved ones, one of my greatest compulsions in life, required thoughtful consideration and planning. I always got a laugh when I said, "I'll put 'be spontaneous' on my calendar for 3:00 p.m."

I gave up control. I was blindsided, and my mother was unstoppable. One morning, in the midst of the turmoil, I called her.

"Richard, I'm glad you called. I've just hung up with the surgeon who I believe should perform the operation you need."

Her voice was calm. She was in charge. She had the facts and a working plan for armor. The woman, whose ironclad will and determination had enabled her to manage four boys under the age of thirteen while getting a master's degree in genetic counseling, had no intention of permitting her son to go unprotected into the darkness.

"We are going to have to schedule surgery to take out your right lung. The procedure is called a pneumonectomy. All the doctors agree. It's quite black and white," she said. "You can live with one lung. You don't really need two. You will be able to breathe normally."

These were the words I was told, and this was what I hung on to. Of course, I didn't really understand it, but I put myself in my mother's extremely capable hands.

My father surprised me. He called me several times a week to see how I was doing and never once mentioned work. He had a checklist of questions about my condition, and after I answered each to his satisfaction, he said, "We are lucky we have your mother to figure out what's best. I know you are safe with her guiding your care, Richard. I am confident you will be all right." Once again, his love for me was routed through his love for her, but I understood that he was extending himself to me as best he could.

The diagnosis and decision to remove my lung happened so fast that I reacted the way I usually reacted to stresses in my life. I worried how this would affect my children. My first impulse was to protect them, but after I gave Jodi the news, she and I decided to be as honest as possible, with an occasional bit of sugarcoating, just as we did with our separation and divorce.

~

We told them one evening when I was home in New Jersey, in the kitchen, this time, because I had already promised them there would be no more bad news in the den. The four of us had dinner together, and I told them to wait before they rushed off for TV and homework.

They looked at me warily, finally having learned that these announcements might not in their best interest.

"We've been through a lot," I said. "I know it. I'm afraid our trials are not over yet. You know I wasn't feeling well when I came back from London and had to have tests in the hospital to see what was wrong with me. Even though there is absolutely nothing wrong with my heart, the doctors did find that my right lung has some evidence of cancer. I'm going to have to have the lung removed, but I'm told—and I believe—that they have found this very, very early, and I am going to be okay."

Michael leaned down and put his head in his hands. He wouldn't look up, and he didn't say a word.

Life Goes On...Thankfully

Rachel seemed to fold in upon herself, getting smaller before my eyes. When she finally looked up at me, her long, thick hair was over her face, and her big eyes were brimming with tears. "How can you say you're going to be okay? Grandpa Lou died of cancer. My Spanish teacher from last year couldn't come back to school because of cancer. You always say everything is going to be okay, and you don't even know for sure! It's not fair!"

Jodi reached over and hugged her. "Rachel, you must listen. Here is the truth. Most people don't get diagnosed with lung cancer until they are very sick, because the people who get sick with this kind of cancer don't have any symptoms until the disease is very advanced. Daddy only found out about it because he had pains in his chest on the plane returning from London. They caught it early."

Michael got up from his seat and began to pace. "How could you get lung cancer?" he shouted. "You don't even smoke! Is this even the truth?"

"Yes, Michael, it's the truth. I've never lied to you, in spite of what you may think, and I'm not lying now. The doctors will take out my right lung but have told me that I will be back to normal as soon as possible. They also said you can lead a full life with just one lung."

This was a fact I was counting on, and one which we repeatedly told our kids. And ourselves.

Once again, I left for New York when they went to bed. I left them with Jodi, knowing she would manage their fears in the best way possible. Again, I realized that it was she who made my life with my children possible, and my gratitude was boundless.

I also had to tell Robert about my diagnosis. He, unfortunately, had had some bad news himself. He had just been fired from his job and was in shock over that. So, we resolved to get through the next few weeks as bravely as possible.

I tried to continue my life in the gray fog between diagnosis and the start of treatment. I went to see *700 Sundays*, a one-man show on Broadway with comedian Billy Crystal. The show was about Billy's life and about his relationship with his father, who died when Billy was thirteen years old. The title was *700 Sundays* because that is the total number of Sundays Crystal had with his dad before he died.

Of course, I couldn't help but wonder how many Sundays Rachel and Michael would have with me after my surgery. It wasn't hard to figure out that if I died from lung cancer, Michael would have had 768 Sundays with me. Rachel would have had 724.

Who would count such a thing? People who lose their parents at a young age, that's who. Michael and Rachel might have to count.

During the past months, as I turned her life upside down by coming out, Rachel had never complained or questioned, at least not to me. She had always saved her tears and worries for Jodi. After our initial conversation about the lung cancer diagnosis, she did not ask me for more details, and I simply repeated to her often that I was sure the doctors would take excellent care of me and that I would be all right.

Rachel and I had a planned trip to California for the days just before the surgery. I decided that I would take her on the trip as planned. I wanted things to be as normal as possible. I heard the therapist's counsel in my head. *If your kids' lives remain normal, they will get through this.*

I figured this advice would apply to my illness as well. I clung to my belief that "normal" was going to sustain my kids, and I had never canceled a trip in my life. So off we went on a five-day father-daughter trip to California in the few weeks between the PET scan and the surgery. We visited friends, swam in the Pacific Ocean, went out for dinner, and toured Universal Studios.

"Dad?" she asked one night when we were alone in the hotel room, watching *Desperate Housewives* on television. "Are you sure you'll be okay?"

She was in her favorite pajamas with the pink-poodle motif, and her eyes were searching mine. She looked beautiful and innocent to me, as always.

Life Goes On...Thankfully

"Yes," I said. "I feel strong, and I intend to follow the doctor's orders to the letter. Plus, they keep telling me that this whole thing was caught early, so I'm going with 'yes, I'll be okay.'"

She seemed reassured once she had the answer she was looking for, and we both went to bed at the same time.

~

I'd had the biopsy at Mount Sinai Hospital two weeks from the day I learned about the suspicious growths. By then, my mother had picked the surgeon, one of the most reputable and respected in the country.

The first order of business was to confirm that the tumors were indeed malignant. In a particular act of rebellion, and of course, denial, I found my voice. I refused to permit the doctor to remove my lung while I was under anesthesia that day, even if the biopsy was quickly tested and left no doubt the growths were cancerous. I wanted to be awake and alert to receive the results of the biopsy before I made my decision. I suppose I still held onto the thought that this was all a mistake, and that my life—so recently upended by my coming out and still so new and precious to me—could be so threatened.

The tumors were malignant. I was diagnosed with non-small cell lung cancer in my right lung. I was forty-four years old. I had never smoked a cigarette in my life, and there was no family history of lung cancer. The decision was made to remove the entire right lung because the tumor, though tiny, had spread across the upper and lower lobes. And though there are three lobes in the right lung, the remaining lobe, which was untouched by the tumors, could not function without the other two.

The next two weeks passed in a whir of activity. We double-checked the treatment plan to remove the right lung with several more surgeons, who all agreed that the best decision would be to remove the entire right lung.

I resumed my relationship with Robert, about whom I was still crazy, and who was still crazy about me. I was discovering that he was also a little crazy, literally. He was given to extremes of love and lust mixed with kindness and unpredictability and occasionally, surprising cruelty.

One night, he revealed a bizarre side I hadn't seen before. He flirted with me and touched me, but he refused to have sex with me. I worried that he might think my cancer was contagious, but he denied that.

He was still the handsomest man I'd ever known, and I was still completely smitten. And now he was out of a job, and I had to have my lung removed. Talk about putting a relationship to the test.

I wanted nothing more than to behave as if there was no threat to my life. I was anxious to get the surgery over and done with so I could return to normal. For the first time ever, I felt my life was unfair, that my vision of "happily ever after" was at risk, and my fate was out of my control. I was starting a love affair that thrilled me despite obvious complications. I had plans for travel, sex, and adventure, and no time for illness. So I squared my shoulders, told myself to hope for the best, and renewed my appreciation for my mother, who was, with her customary skill, thoroughness, and intelligence, taking the lead on my medical care and guiding me through the morass.

The night before the surgery to remove my lung, I took a client out for dinner and a show on Broadway. We saw *The Producers*, with Nathan Lane and Matthew Broderick. It was one of my favorites, with an impossible, happy ending. I had seen the show before with Jodi. I did not tell her I was going to see it again the night before the operation. I did not tell the client anything about my impending surgery. I just wanted to pretend that everything was as normal as possible.

Sitting in the theater, I played a mental game I have played many times since. I looked around, scrutinizing the people in the audience. Many were from out of town, some were gay, most were straight, and all had their own life stories to tell, I was certain. But I would bet that none of them was having a lung removed in the morning.

What I did not understand then, even though I kept mouthing the words to my kids, was that I really was lucky. The doctors had genuinely caught it early, before it could spread to other parts of my body. Surgery, not chemotherapy, was the right way to go. My cancer was contained. The mysterious terrible chest pains had truly saved my life.

Seventeen

Bracelet of Needles

"Living with Lung Cancer"

We stand on either side of the hospital bed,
And gaze at our son. His eyes are shut.
At dawn he was whole, but now he is not.
Where two lungs resided, there is one instead.
With each labored breath, through a tube and a mask,
Only one side of his chest expands and then contracts.
Toward each of us he lifts an arm with its bracelet of needles.
His slumber is drugged, yet he knows we are there.
Though our hearts are fractured, we murmur our love.
With his eyes still closed, he smiles.

~Audrey Heimler

My mother wrote that poem on May 20, 2004. I don't remember much about the day of the operation. I was filled with morphine and an overdose of denial. But I do know this: I thought my ordeal was over when they took out my lung. I had made my deal with the devil—one lung in exchange for a return to normalcy. I was determined to get back to my new life.

My children were uppermost in my mind. We had been as honest as possible; but hearing that a person can lead a full life with just one lung and seeing me in the bed after the surgery were two different things. So we held off on their visit until I was out of the ICU and off the ventilator.

Life Goes On...Thankfully

Any patient soon learns that there are staff members with whom they feel simpatico and those with whom they don't. I waited till my favorite nurse came in.

"My kids are coming," I told her, "and I want to look as normal as possible. So can we cover up these wires and tubes?"

"The wires are where they are, I'm afraid, and there's not much we can do about it."

I felt a surge of despair. She was not on board with my vision. I had to convince her. I would not let them see me looking so sick. If I looked okay, they would believe I was okay.

I recalled a movie I had seen many years earlier, when I was just about their age. It was called *Papillon* and starred Dustin Hoffman and Steve McQueen. They were prisoners in a terrible jail on a remote island, where they were endlessly mistreated, both in solitary confinement in cells next to one another. They would tap on the walls of their cells to send each other messages. At one point, they were allowed to stick their heads out of air holes cut in their tiny cells to get some sunlight and see each other. They looked terrible, with squinty, blinking eyes, grisly beards, sunken cheeks, and rotting teeth.

"How do I look?" each asked the other.

"You look good; you look fine," each said.

They knew that when a person is on death's doorstep, if he looks good, he has a better chance of survival.

I wanted to look good for my children. I wanted that visual more than anything else. I wanted them to feel safe, not terrified that I was dying.

"Humor me, please," I said. "My kids have just gone through the separation of their parents. Having their father get lung cancer is just too much."

"All right, then. We'll see what we can do."

The nurse combed my hair, remade my bed, and brought in extra blankets to cover my wires as much as possible. She helped me brush my teeth and cleaned me up. She made me look and feel presentable. I felt overwhelmed by her kindness.

When my kids came, Jodi was there, too, along with my mother, and somehow we all got through that first visit. It wasn't a party, but it wasn't a wake, either. Michael hugged me carefully and said he thought I looked pretty good.

Rachel, looking frightened, carried a Boston Chicken takeout bag. She had insisted that Jodi stop on the way to the hospital so she could buy me one of my favorites—a chicken sandwich. Jodi agreed, even though she knew the doctors would never let me eat it.

Rachel visibly brightened when she saw me and gave me my present. "Dad! I was so worried about you! How do you feel? You actually look okay!"

"Not bad for an old man," I said. "Wait till you see me walk with an IV pole—fastest man in the hallway."

Things were off to a good start, and I began to relax. They didn't stay long, but it was long enough for me to put my best foot forward as we all maneuvered through our once-again altered universe. I was still going to be the irreverent father they knew and loved, gay or straight, two lungs or one.

~

The next day, Robert came to visit me. When he entered the room, I felt a surge of excitement and then a rush of embarrassment. He was so gorgeous, vibrant, and healthy, and I felt sick and skeletal, with prominent bones and tubes everywhere. It was an odd juxtaposition, the glamorous new boyfriend and his one-lung lover.

"Hello, gorgeous," I said, stealing Barbra Streisand's best line in *Funny Girl*.

"Hello yourself." He came directly over to the bed, took my hand, and kissed me on the lips.

I could see immediately that he had a side I'd never experienced before, so busy was I with the sex, the heat, and the bewilderment of the love I felt. He could actually be compassionate, too.

"I want to come and take care of you," he said. "I don't have a job right now, so why not?"

I could think of no reason at all.

Immediately after he uttered the words, Jodi walked into the room with a spray of flowers and some *rugulah*. She took one look at Robert, came over to my bed, and kissed me on the lips. It was my second kiss on the lips of the day and generated much more complex emotions than the first one had. This kiss was from my ex-wife, ex-lover, and the mother of my children. It was her way of letting me—and perhaps Robert—know that marital bonds are not so easily broken, and she was not yet done with her vow to love me in sickness and in health.

But the recovery plan remained intact. When I was discharged, Robert came to my apartment and took care of me. He was thoughtful and tender. He cooked for me, gave me my meds, and lay next to me while we watched television. He helped me shower and take my first steps outdoors with one lung. I was deeply grateful and completely enamored.

One post-op day, Robert and I went out walking together down West End Avenue. My parents, Jodi, Michael, and Rachel were walking toward us, coming to visit me. We all went upstairs and were soon joined by my friend Gary from Philadelphia, my first gay obsession, and his new partner, Russ.

I could never have imagined this gathering just a year earlier. I understood that my illness had pulled everyone together in the same room. Everyone was getting along. We were all pushed, like it or not, into a new place. They say whatever doesn't kill you makes you stronger. And that's where we were that day. Stronger.

I began to return to my life, at first with some hesitation, but then with growing confidence that it was still *my* life. You really can breathe with only one lung. I had the prescribed physical therapy, respiratory therapy, and the follow-up appointments with my new slew of doctors. I went back to work and back to my routine, bit by bit. Sometimes I forgot that I only had one lung. Robert stayed with me, and our relationship seemed to deepen while I was still fragile.

But as I grew stronger, I could feel him pulling away. He blamed it on his disquiet over not having a job and feeling unsure about his future. I was still in love, though, and desperate to hang on to this first love of mine. I convinced him that, in time, perhaps I could help him find work, but that I really needed him during my recovery. I was busy with healthcare follow-ups, pulmonary therapy, and just regaining my strength. I was optimistic that my pneumonectomy would not significantly alter my life. My friends had gathered round, both gay and straight, and I was told I could still ski and travel. I thought I had dodged a bullet.

I loved having Robert around, but it was clear to me even in my distracted state that he needed a new job. He needed to go back to work. A friend of mine was able to make a referral for him in Washington, DC, and Robert got a new job as a result. He and I began a long-distance relationship, which was the best we could do under the circumstances.

Six months later, I took Michael on a trip to England. Michael had always been a sports fanatic, and we always had special events to go to, whether it was a football game at my alma mater, Northwestern, or one at his college, the University of Wisconsin. He was also a huge tennis fan, and I'd gotten some tickets at a cancer fund raiser for a special tour of Wimbledon. He was ecstatic. I felt strong enough to go, and I proceeded with my plan to live my life as if I had never gotten cancer.

While the two of us were in London, I began to feel strangely weak. I was battling an exhaustion that I had never felt before in my life. I did not tell Michael, and I did not let it curtail our trip, but I felt the threat of illness.

When I returned home, I was still not feeling well. No matter how little I exerted myself, I couldn't seem to catch my breath.

I went with my brother Ronnie to see a gastro pulmonologist on the Upper West Side of New York, near my apartment. The doctor tested me and told me my oxygen levels were fine. He could find no reason for my shortness of breath and dismissed me. But even as I was leaving his office building, I suddenly had no strength to walk.

"Something's not right," I kept saying to Ronnie. "I can't walk, and I can't breathe." My heart was yammering away in my chest, more from panic than anything else. Ronnie sat me down in the lobby of the building.

Neither of us knew what to do next. I had been told I was fine, literally minutes earlier. But clearly, I was not.

I kept staring at the marble walls of the lobby, trying to breathe, trying to calm myself down and understand what was happening to me.

"Let me call Mom and Dad," Ronnie said. "They're probably almost here."

My parents were on their way in to New York to visit because they knew I hadn't been feeling well. Ronnie called them, knowing they could get me home faster than a cab would, if they were close by. And in fact, they were just minutes away, but by the time they arrived, I could barely get up from my chair in the lobby.

They loaded me into the car, and I sipped from a water bottle that my mother had brought. Suddenly, I began to gag. "I can't breathe!" I said. The noises coming from my body were terrifying.

It took several seconds, but my mother reacted first. "We have to call 911. He's choking!"

It seemed like only an instant before we heard the blare of sirens and three medics descended upon us with medical equipment and assurances that everything was going to be okay.

Suddenly, I was on the way to Columbia Presbyterian Hospital in a screaming ambulance with an oxygen mask on my face. I remember the sickening sensation of not being able to get enough air. I remember sputtering and panicking. I remember being admitted to the ER, and then everything went black.

I woke up three days later with no memory of the time that had gone by. I had come closer to death than ever before in my life.

I learned I had sustained six, count 'em, *six* cardiac arrests. I was in the ICU at Columbia, wired up all over again, this time with a tube in my throat that prevented me from speaking.

I remembered nothing at first, but later I recalled moments of pure terror. I couldn't eat, I couldn't sleep, I couldn't drink, I couldn't speak. I felt claustrophobic. People were putting wet, cold popsicle sticks on my parched lips, but I couldn't tell if it was family or staff. The only words I remember were "leave the lights on," but I don't really know if I said them or not. I was terrified of darkness and death.

I remember my friend and attorney, Jeff, sitting in my room. There were nurses there, too, signing papers, acting as witnesses. Apparently there were some loose legal ends in my will, and Jeff wanted me to sign some papers. They were certain I was going to die.

But I surprised them all. I continued to fight for my life, and slowly, I began to win.

A week or so after I was admitted, I began communicating by writing notes on a yellow legal pad. I asked for clarity. I remembered nothing. What happened to me? Did I have a cardiac arrest? What meds was I on? Then, as I began to feel stronger, "How is Michael? How is Rachel? What do they know?"

One brilliant doctor, Dr. Joshua Sonett, a thoracic surgeon at Columbia Presbyterian Hospital, figured out what was wrong with me and designed a groundbreaking surgical procedure that saved my life.

Apparently, after my lung was removed, my other body parts began to shift into the vacuum that was created in my chest cavity. My spine, which was already curved because of my childhood scoliosis, had been slowly moving into the space where my lung had been and was crushing my esophagus. The doctor discovered that bony protrusions of my spine had poked a hole in my esophagus, creating a huge leak that made it impossible for the air that I was breathing to efficiently enter my one remaining lung.

Life Goes On...Thankfully

Dr. Sonett devised a unique plan. He essentially packed my empty chest cavity with silicone breast implants to take up the space where my lung had been. He repaired the hole in my esophagus, and he sutured my esophagus back where it belonged.

I was discharged from the hospital after ten days, shortly before Thanksgiving. We were going to celebrate the holiday. Thanksgiving had taken on a new meaning. I was thankful for my life and for the people around me who had gotten me through. But I also recognized there was no more denying the insidiousness of the enemy within my body. I knew I was going to change my life yet again.

~

Six months later, I retired from the family business. While I was proud of everything we had done, we had to admit that the business was dying. Manufacturing had shifted from the United States to Asia, and the retail business had become savaged by competition from national chain stores. Our company, which had enabled three generations of Heimlers to support their families, was outdated, a relic of the past, a dinosaur facing certain extinction. Our once successful business was one more in a wave of falling dominos unable to compete in the new global economy.

Because of my illness, I was a candidate for short- and long-term disability, which, with my savings, was enough to enable me to support myself without the business. Without having to pay my salary, my brothers could remain in the business a bit longer as well, although they, too, had to figure out where they wanted to be in the future when the business could no longer sustain them.

I thought often of my friend and mentor, Leonard Fein, the social activist who encouraged living a life with larger meaning. I took his words to heart again, aware now that my time on this earth was more precious and more important to me than ever before. I began to think seriously of working in the Jewish nonprofit sector, an area in which I had always had an intense interest, and I began a job search.

I also decided to redouble my efforts as an advocate for the lung cancer community. When I was first diagnosed with lung cancer, I volunteered with the American Lung Association and was asked to support lung cancer victims who wanted to talk about their diagnoses with others. I was given the name of a man who was in prison for murder on Riker's Island, New York. I corresponded with him for two years. The task felt painful to me, not at all rewarding, because I didn't understand him nor could he understand me.

Our correspondence was stilted, labored, and probably harder for me than for him. He was a poor, unfortunate person with a history of bad judgment and a crescendo of bad luck that ended with a prison sentence and a lung cancer diagnosis. I was wholly unequipped to help him, but I felt someone had to do it—a symptom of my Best Little Boy syndrome. Via email, I gave him information about his illness, tried to understand his life, and offered him encouragement. Then, one day, he asked me to buy him a television set. I balked. The chasm felt too wide. I bought him the television, and then I never wrote back again. It was one of the few jobs I ever quit.

I decided to try again, and I joined the newly restructured Lung Cancer Alliance to help create public policy and raise funds for lung cancer research. I hoped to add something meaningful to the effort to help those stricken with this deadly disease. I wanted to believe that I could really make a difference.

Sadly, my new life did not include Robert. He and I had broken up. He was both wonderful and unpredictable, with hot flashes of uncontrolled and explosive anger. He took care of me after I was discharged from the hospital and revealed a tender, generous soul I had not known existed. After he got his new job in Washington, we saw each other frequently at first, but work and obligations seemed to get in the way of routine visits. Then, it became clear that we were no longer going to be able to sustain our relationship.

When he first moved to Washington, he found a temporary apartment. But right after my second surgery, he bought a condominium on the fourth floor of a building with no elevator, all without talking to me about it. I was unable to walk more than a block or two at the time, let alone climb a set of stairs. That passive-aggressive cruelty caused me so much stress that I knew this was no longer a relationship I could continue. Although he had been a wonderful caretaker after my surgery, the relationship could not sustain itself.

I became a dating machine.

Eighteen

Frogs and Princes

Rules and Surprises When Dating with Lung Cancer
1. Never tell about a lung cancer diagnosis on the first date. The third date, if there is one, is soon enough.
2. Nurses make excellent dates. They are compassionate and good people.
3. Look for a spark. Don't settle. Ever. At least, try not to.
4. You have to kiss a lot of frogs before you meet a prince.

One could say that all the dating was shallow, but the truth is, I just went right back to my earliest desires. I wanted to find true love, and I did not want to settle for anything less. So, since I didn't like to drink alcohol, I went to Starbucks (or as Samantha on *Sex in the City* called it, Starfucks), where I conducted speed dates with guys I met over the internet, drinking endless cups of passion fruit tea. I sifted through countless strangers to find the right man with the right spark. I interviewed so often—sometimes three men a night—that I embarrassed even myself. Sometimes just one look was enough to pass immediately (but politely), and sometimes I tried to convince myself a guy was sexy or funny or interesting. But mostly not.

And then, I met Paul.

Paul was a nurse. He was the first guy I really liked after the whole debacle with Robert. Paul was cute, a little baldish, with an impish smile, and a muscled, compact body. His voice and mannerisms were a bit effeminate, which was not appealing to me, as I really preferred the tall, dark, handsome, stoic type, but I didn't want to cross him off the list based on that alone. He was easy to talk with, funny, and warm. I waited till the second date, which was a dinner, forfeiting my three-date rule before the all-important news flash.

"I have to tell you something." I twisted my iced-tea straw into a tight, little knot. "I'm a lung cancer survivor. I only have one lung, but I'm okay now."

"Really?" Without missing a beat, Paul countered. "Funny coincidence. I had testicular cancer."

He didn't care that I had lung cancer, and as a nurse, he knew full well, probably better than I did, the grim statistics for lung cancer survivors. Testicular cancer was mostly a curable disease.

My time with Paul was healing time. He was sweet and soothing, where Robert had been movie-star gorgeous, electrifying, and cruel. Paul was a salve to my wounds, a kind, wonderful soul with whom I spent a blissful summer on Fire Island, trying to get to whatever normal was going to be. Paul was the first man who loved me and my kids, whom he welcomed to his Fire Island home as if they were his own.

Fire Island had cachet. It was seductive, with its prohibition of cars, long lovely beaches, and cute red wagons we all used to transport groceries to the house and whatever we needed to the beach. It was high on the cool factor, and my kids loved going there despite its reputation as a heavily gay New York beach. There were bonfires on the beach, lots of barbecues in the setting sun, and in general, a feeling of great relaxation and entitlement.

Paul and I had plenty of privacy and a lot of sex in his house. But after a relatively short time, I began to feel that the sex would not sustain me for the long run. And I was still a novice in the gay world. Paul was the most effeminate man I had ever dated, which made me uncomfortable when he was with my children and my straight friends. I could not overcome the feelings of disquiet, and I ended that relationship when the summer was over.

"You used me!" he said, when I told him that despite all, it was over. "You liked me well enough when you were in my house on Fire Island and your kids could come! Suddenly, now, it's over?"

He was livid, and I could understand why. But I couldn't help it. I knew I had made a mistake, and I was ashamed that I had indeed taken advantage of his hospitality and generous soul. I thought he was fun, sexy, and certainly understanding about my illness, but I was certain we were finished. I wanted to be honest, and I thought a quick, honest breakup was the least harmful course.

What I wanted more than anything else was another eighteen-year relationship like the one I had with Jodi, only this time, with the right man. Paul was not the one.

Life Goes On...Thankfully

A Letter of Life

April 12, 2006
To my friends and family,

Today I recognize and celebrate the second anniversary of my lung cancer diagnosis. In some ways, it seems like more than two years and in other ways, I can still feel the confusion of the unknown when I heard the words "there is a spot on your lung."

I know many people celebrate the day their doctor said they were "cancer free." I choose to acknowledge the day I was diagnosed because it is the day that changed my life forever. I also do not believe a cancer survivor is ever cancer-free; we are "living with cancer" every day of our lives.

I share this letter this year with my new friends at the Lung Cancer Alliance and the Jewish Outreach Institute. I was honored to join the New York chapter of the LCA, a very important advocacy organization. I have met a wonderful group of passionate professionals, cancer survivors, and family members of cancer patients. We hope in the years ahead to change the perception of lung cancer, to raise awareness with our government and the media, and to generate research interest for this deadly disease.

I recently watched the closing ceremony of the 2006 Winter Olympics and witnessed the quadriplegic mayor of Vancouver accept and wave the Olympic flag as the leader of the next city that will host the games. He said his "disability was a career opportunity." I can say the same thing about my health issue. I am very fortunate to have a fulfilling new career with the welcoming, energetic, and devoted staff of the Jewish Outreach Institute.

Dana Reeve, who recently passed away from lung cancer, said that "life is not always fair, but it can still be worthwhile." I truly believe those words, and this past year was very worthwhile and memorable for me. I had the joy of celebrating Rachel's Sweet 16 with Jodi, Michael, and one hundred of Rachel's closest friends. And I had the surreal and emotional experience of moving Michael into his dorm room at the University of Wisconsin in Madison. Go, Badgers!

The best news of all is that my doctors are pleased with my test results, and my prognosis is very positive. I felt great for the entire year, and I even gained thirty-eight pounds. I will miss having Mrs. Fields cookies, Swiss Miss pudding, and Ben & Jerry's ice cream as my evening snack. (Yes, all three in the same night.)

Please know as I begin the third year of my journey that each of you are my therapy and my medication. Thank you for making me believe I am still me.

Enjoy your holidays this week. All my love, now and forever,
Richard

Nineteen

Modern Family

Two men were sitting together in a gay bar after connecting on the internet. They were getting along famously. One was tall, dark-haired, slender, and handsome, with a quick wit and a propensity to laugh. He also had half his chest cavity stuffed with breast implants.

The other was tall, too, but rounder, a little hefty, pleasant enough, but not someone you would pick out of a lineup as remarkably good-looking. He was dressed expensively, and he had a kind face with intelligent eyes. He was obviously interested in the man across the table from him. They were laughing, totally engaged with each other.

The big guy, whose eyes were crinkling with laughter, was on the receiving end of a pop quiz.

"What is your favorite baseball team? Have you ever had sex with a sports star? What is your favorite Broadway show? Have you ever stalked an actor?" He'd fielded all those questions and was ready for more.

"Do you like to travel? (If the answer is no, the date will be over.)" I said. "Where have you been?"

"Everywhere," said the big guy. "I'm an antiques dealer, and I buy products all over the world."

"What is on your bucket list?"

"Dubai."

"What is your favorite cereal?"

"Fruit Loops. Don't judge me."

The next day, I dropped off a carton of milk and a box of Fruit Loops at David's apartment building. I gave it all to the doorman, with a big tip and explicit instructions to find a refrigerator.

The day after that, we met for lunch. I was feeling the electrical excitement of another spark, the initial tumultuous feeling that I might have met someone really special. I found myself humming "Something's Comin'" from the scene in *West Side Story* in which Tony meets Maria at the dance and gets hooked.

I was not going to tell David about the lung cancer until the third date. But, then, during our lunch, he told me his mother had a brain tumor and his father had lung cancer. They were still alive, but cancer had ravaged them both.

My first thought was why would he want to date me? Who wants to have a mother, a father, *and* a boyfriend all battling cancer?

So, I broke my rule. He was so charismatic and honest and clearly dedicated to helping his parents battle their own illnesses. I couldn't lie or be secretive. I just put it out there. "I have something in common with your father," I said. "Lung cancer. I had a lung removed two years ago and some recurrences since. I can understand if you've had your fill."

He didn't even flinch. "I'll tell you what. Why don't we just take it one day at a time and see what happens?"

And just like that, the relationship was off and running.

~

David lived a very extravagant life. His exquisite, three-bedroom Park Avenue apartment had been in his family for decades and was studded with gilded antiques, jades, silk drapes, and crystal chandeliers. When I first visited I surprised myself by feeling intimidated, so I fought back with flippancy.

"David. I'm lost. I thought I was on Park Avenue in New York, but now I realize I'm in an episode of *Antiques Roadshow*."

His honest response surprised me. "You've already stolen my heart, but you have still to prove you're not here to steal anything else…"

David was not comfortable with that kind of humor. He cherished his collectibles and, as I began to understand, was a very private person who was not used to inviting a new lover to his prized lair.

It was a few weeks before he told me that he also had a rustic, magnificently furnished house in the country, a few hours from New York, stocked with equally rare and breathtaking antiques.

David was a master at his craft. He knew the provenance and value of every piece and selected for his own residences only things he really loved and valued. He was one of the few people I'd met who had traveled more extensively than I had. He was always on the cusp of the next exciting journey.

David was fiercely independent, accomplished, and razor smart. He was an expert in a world I knew nothing about. He had recently purchased his great-uncle's antique business, a respected boutique firm that had worked with first ladies in the White House. He understood art history and specialized in antique furnishings and lighting fixtures. Where I lost myself in the staging of a theatrical production, David was a set designer of a different sort, who could unearth and showcase artifacts from around the world, giving them renewed stature and prominence.

David was Jewish. He understood my deep connection to my religion and my love for my children and family. I fell for him, hard and fast.

Shortly after we met, the Jewish High Holy Days were imminent. That meant three days in the temple and lots of family time. Unbeknown to me, David called Jodi at home in New Jersey.

"Jodi," he said. "I'm calling to see how you would feel about me coming to your synagogue in Wyckoff for the High Holidays. I'd like to be with Richard, and I want to get to know Michael and Rachel because Richard loves them so much. But I won't go if you don't feel comfortable with it."

Jodi, generous and openhearted as always, agreed. Because of her, David was welcomed into the bosom of our family. He assumed his seat in my pantheon of stars as my first Jewish boyfriend, the man I had been hoping to find all my life—or, at least, since I'd come out.

David's entry into my life was the start of our version of the modern family—the gay dad; the sophisticated, rich, gay boyfriend; the ex-wife and kids, and the loving and quirky extended family. I got to know his father and his two "uncles" (one was natural, and one was his uncle's partner), both in their nineties, who had started the antique business many decades earlier. Philip and Roy had had a surprisingly long, fulfilling relationship. Philip was dapper and always well dressed, managing to sport a bow tie and get away with it. He was a raconteur with a treasure trove of stories about old New York salons and society. He had started the antiques company that distinguished the homes of the upper crust of New York and established a national reputation for himself.

Roy was quieter but whip smart. He was an expert bridge player and wrote a syndicated newspaper column on bridge strategy. He was a linguist who spoke French and Spanish fluently and had fantastic memories of his worldwide travels despite his age. Both men had succeeded in their long relationship in a decidedly gay-unfriendly world. Despite all the odds, they had made their lives and their love work. They were inspiring to me.

My parents embraced my relationship with David. Soon after they met him at synagogue over the Jewish holidays, they went to David's apartment for one of his spectacular home-cooked meals. To my surprise, he got along very well with my father. There seemed to be none of the distance I felt in my own relationship with him. If anything, David seemed less comfortable around my mother, with whom I had always felt so close.

I was proud to introduce David to my friends, and soon we began to spend all of our time together. I gave up my apartment and moved in with him, since I was spending all my time there anyway. At first, I tiptoed around a lot, giving those antiques a wide berth, but eventually I got used to living on half tiptoe. We traveled widely together, antiquing our way through France and Italy, and even made it to David's bucket-list location, Dubai. What a place that was! It was Disneyland on steroids, studded with high-rises that literally pierced the clouds and an upper class that knew no fiscal boundaries.

I thought I was a big spender until I met David. He could spend breathtaking sums if he fell in love with an antique or curio or painting, and he was comfortable with the financial risks he took. He was confident that he could sell his newest find—and mostly, he was right. Sometimes he called a client from a faraway shop or market and sent a picture and a buy recommendation and got a go-ahead to purchase.

"Hey, I sold jewels, too," I said. Except mine were fake, and the clients were nothing like the sophisticates in David's book of buyers.

When I moved in with him, I nurtured the hope that this was the relationship that would make my all dreams come true. I could be with him and my kids, my parents, and my friends. David understood me. He had no kids of his own, and he responded to mine with warmth and inclusion. He willingly took Rachel on a vacation with us and soon cared for her deeply. He understood Michael, respected his reticence, and did his best to be kind to him. He even attended Michael's college graduation with me.

When Michael began to look for work in Manhattan, I wanted him to live with us in New York until he got a job. David welcomed Michael, but set his own rules, which were stricter than mine would ever have been. He offered Michael the pullout couch in the den and the nightly use of the guest bathroom, but he made it a condition of residence that Michael close up the sofa bed every morning and return the den and the bathroom to pristine condition. Michael, who had been a typical college slob, was not used to such fastidious conditions. But he pulled up his socks (literally) and obliged.

David, whose fastidiousness extended into food, often prepared his own lunch to take with him to his office when he was not dining with clients. He was an early advocate of eating nothing but the finest foods, and he preferred his own brand of BYO to quick purchases in New York's sandwich shops. He loved to share his passions and one day surprised me when he offered the same to Michael.

"I'm happy to prepare some extra food for you to take to your job, Mike. New York lunches can add up pretty quickly."

"No thanks," Mike said, eyeing a terrine of pate on the counter in front of David. "I'm good."

But after a few days of buying astronomically expensive sandwiches in New York's cheapest delis, Mike said to David over breakfast, "Would you really make me lunch? Lunch costs twenty dollars, and I've had better food in cafeterias. I started going to food trucks, but they are making me kind of sick..."

David laughed. "I'd love to, Mike. And don't worry, you don't have to eat everything I do. I'll pick up some roast beef and other cold cuts at Eli's on Madison Avenue, so you'll have plenty to eat that you like."

I had to laugh to myself. I knew the prices at Eli's. I would never have gone in there for cold cuts, even for my son. But I kept my mouth shut, glad to see they were creating their own give and take.

They bonded over wine as well. David loved wine, and to my surprise, Michael did as well, and they talked about the flavors, the aromas, and the regions with a surprising variety of descriptive phrases I found amusing—though I was careful not to show it. Grassy? Smoky? Robust? Buttery? Hint of asparagus? Good for Michael. I always pictured Michael as more of a beer drinker, so I was surprised that he actually liked wine and liked to talk about it, but I was so happy they had found their first footing.

~

Life Goes On...Thankfully

After I explored my options for a job in the nonprofit sector, I landed a position as a development director for an organization called Jewish Outreach Institute. Its mission was to help make the Jewish community more welcoming to interfaith families. At the time, that was a novel concept, and I wanted very much to be a part of it. I was finally in a place in my life where I could do something I loved for something I believed in.

The organization placed a lot of faith in me, despite my lack of direct experience. When I took the job, I wasn't sure I could really do it right, but no one else seemed to be worried. I certainly believed in the mission. I wanted to help interfaith families find a home in synagogues that had not yet accepted intermarriage as a Jewish way of life. I felt strongly that Jewish people who fell in love with non-Jews and wanted to participate in Jewish life should not be excluded because ancient Jewish laws prohibited intermarriage.

I also loved my work as an advocate in the battle against lung cancer. I wanted to help fight the disease that had struck me out of nowhere and was more deadly than the five most common cancers combined. The New York-based Lung Cancer Alliance welcomed me. That organization was reorganizing its leadership and looking for additional help. I already knew and respected the organization enough to have made a substantial donation.

Soon after my diagnosis and just after I came out of the closet, there was a cancer fund raiser at Temple Beth Rishon in Wyckoff, New Jersey, with me as the honoree. All my friends and family came for a giant Sunday walk-a-thon called "Cure Ahead." I jokingly dubbed it a belated coming out party/premature funeral but in fact, it was fantastic. We raised almost $100,000 that day, which was a sum then unheard of for our small synagogue in New Jersey.

When I stood up to say a few words before the entire congregation at the start of the walk, I saw a sea of yellow T-shirts emblazoned with the optimistic message "Cure Ahead," and I felt the love in the room. This was a way for everyone I knew to show support, and even though I was uncomfortable receiving all the attention, I felt so happy to raise this kind of money in the battle against lung cancer.

I gave the contribution to the Lung Cancer Alliance. Its mission was to create a national voice and a legislative presence for lung cancer, both of which were sorely needed. I knew full well that money for a cure was not all we needed; we needed a full-on public relations battle for the interim period.

Whenever I told people I was diagnosed with lung cancer and had one lung removed, I could practically hear their brains ticking as they asked the next question. "Did you smoke?"

I did not smoke. Neither did 30 percent of other lung-cancer victims, but I began to see that people are so afraid of cancer that they search for a reason why they won't get it too. And when I undermined that defense just by being who I was, they immediately recoiled from me, even on a subconscious level, fearful that they, too, could get this disease.

Celebrities such as George Harrison, Steve McQueen, John Wayne, Donna Summer, Paul Newman, Dana Reeve, and Peter Jennings, whose fame could be leveraged to help raise funds to fight lung cancer, would not come forth openly about the cancer that eventually killed them. That information was deliberately omitted from some of their obituaries. It bothered me that my diagnosis of lung cancer implied that I had done something wrong. Living with cancer also meant overcoming shame, a double challenge that could slay the staunchest of us.

And of course, I had had plenty of experience with shame. I found myself jealous of the successes of the AIDS community and breast cancer victims. They had all suffered, undeniably, but they had gotten their day in the sun, beaten the odds, and gotten the funding required to help develop a cure for the majority of victims.

Lung cancer, the biggest killer of all, had none of that. More people get lung cancer than breast, colon, prostate, and cervical cancer combined. The worst part is that lung cancer is a silent, stealthy killer. Most people don't get diagnosed until it has already spread through their bodies.

Life Goes On...Thankfully

I wanted to be part of an organization that was helping to change the negative image of lung cancer, raise awareness, shape public policy on the disease, and advance the options for research and federal funding. At the time, the only public health policy that existed for lung cancer victims was a campaign to stop smoking. No amount of private funding was going to provide the resources so desperately needed. What we wanted were federal funds and a completely new image. We needed to take a page out of the AIDS and breast cancer movement playbooks and learn how to fight to get the resources needed for a real battle against this killer. It seemed like a worthwhile way to spend my life.

I befriended Laurie Fenton, one of the leaders of the Lung Cancer Alliance. She was a small, sweet-faced woman with a huge mind and a winning personality. She had a public policy background and knew how to get into the halls of Congress to speak with the people who created new public policy. She asked me to join her as an advocate in Congress, and I accepted. Little did I understand how passionate and tirelessly committed she was. On our first trip to Washington, DC, she marched me endlessly around the halls of Congress. It pushed the resources of my remaining lung, but I was thrilled to have the opportunity to make substantive change. I knew that my presence was essential. I was the face of lung cancer for the decision-makers. I knew that my story resonated with people, both because I could reach out and speak effectively and because so many had been touched in some way by the disease.

One day, the indefatigable Laurie made appointments with what felt like every legislator and advocate in Washington. Finally, hoping for a ten-minute break, I stopped her. "Laurie," I said. "You're killing me. You forgot that I already had lung cancer. I only have one lung. I can't keep up this pace!"

But I did. I went gladly, willingly, and with the best intentions. I often thought of my favorite song from the Broadway show *Pippin*, and the lyric, "I want my life to be something more than long."

The child who always wanted to be the best little boy in the world had an unexpected opportunity to shine when he grew up and faced lung cancer. I became an advocate for drug companies whose miracle drugs were beginning to change the course of the disease. For too long, the treatments available for lung cancer victims were the standards—chemotherapy, radiation, and surgery. Over time, though, the drug companies began to offer clinical trials for drugs in development—drugs that helped save my life in clinical trials. I spoke to the sales teams at pharmaceutical giants Pfizer, Abbott, and Novartis , whose job it was to go out and raise awareness about the drugs in development so that doctors around the country could prescribe them for patients. I traveled to distant cities to speak in front of hundreds of drug company staffers. Of course, I would always get nervous, but usually the audience reacted strongly. After all, most of us want to do a good job at work, and my speeches reminded the sales teams that the drugs they worked so hard to sell actually saved lives. "Because of you," I told them, "I was able to go to my son's college graduation. Because of you, I hope to one day dance at my fifteen-year-old daughter's wedding."

My mother went to one of those sales meetings with me. "Richard," she said, when I was done speaking, "There wasn't a dry eye in the house."

Twenty

A Weekend Call

Cancer patients learn quickly the rigors of waiting for test results. I was on a regular schedule of brain MRIs and CAT scans because lung cancer frequently metastasizes to the brain before traveling elsewhere. That meant a lot of anxiety between the time I had a test and the time I got the results.

I learned to be hypersensitive to the slightest facial expression, verbal cue, or body language from the many healthcare professionals who administered and reported the results of my tests. That's a survival instinct at its most honed. The least little tipoff—a frown, a false smile, a flicker of uncertainty in a response—would set me off, worrying that I was in trouble. Telephone calls from nurses or physician's assistants were usually good news. Calls from the oncologist were not. Weekend calls were the worst.

David, who had many times taken both of his parents to doctors and hospitals for tests and follow-ups for their cancers said it best. "They never call you on a Sunday to see how your weekend is going."

One Sunday in October 2006, Dr. Stoopler called me. It was a gorgeous autumn morning and the leaves outside were ablaze with vibrant color. I was sitting on the sofa in David's country house in the Catskills. We were going back to New York shortly to attend services for Yom Kippur, the Day of Atonement, the holiest day of the Jewish calendar. This is the time God decides each person's fate, so we make amends and ask forgiveness for all of our sins of the previous year.

I would be dropping David off in New York, where he was to catch a plane to Arizona to visit his parents, and I was planning to attend services at my temple in Wyckoff that evening with Jodi, Michael, Rachel, and my parents. I'd been asked to give the Kol Nidre address to the congregation, which is one of the highest honors the temple can bestow upon a congregant. My speech was already written. It was a mix of inspirational messages and gratitude. I would speak about the importance of the synagogue in our lives and my appreciation for the tremendous support the members of the synagogue had provided since my illness began.

Then I saw Dr. Stoopler's name and number on my caller ID. It was a Sunday, a few days after my most recent brain scan. In that glance, that brief second, I knew my life was about to change.

Dr. Stoopler was his usual friendly but succinct self. "Richard, I'm calling to tell you that your brain scan showed evidence of a growth. The cancer has spread. We are going to have to operate to remove the tumor."

It was the worst thing I could possibly have heard. For some reason, "brain tumor" felt devastating, worse than lung cancer.

He offered encouragement, but I was listening to the sound of my heart beating, and I had trouble focusing on his words.

"Come in to see me on Tuesday, after the holiday. We'll schedule the surgery with a very good brain surgeon, Dr. Bruce. I believe the tumor is small, and the surgery will be successful. It's a setback, but you're strong, and you will recover."

But all I heard was "brain cancer." I thought of my friend, Murray Prawer, who died of a brain tumor. He had a headache that wouldn't go away. He got an MRI, they found a glioblastoma, and he was gone. I never thought I would get a brain tumor. It was my worst fear.

I hung up the phone. David was in the house, but I didn't tell him. He was getting ready for his flight to Arizona to visit his parents, both of whom were debilitated by cancer themselves, and I knew he would never leave if I told him my news. There was plenty of time for that when he returned. I just wanted to get out of there before I collapsed.

I composed myself and went upstairs to our bedroom, where he was packing. "Let's go," I said. "We'll probably hit some traffic. I have to drop you at the airport, and I'd just as soon get started."

"So early? What's the sudden rush?"

"I'm nervous about my speech. In fact, why don't you drive? If you can stand it, I'll practice out loud while you're at the wheel."

Somehow, in a haze of anxiety, after I dispatched David in New York, I made it to New Jersey. I went to Jodi's house, where Jodi, Michael, Rachel, and I would meet my parents before we all went to synagogue.

I had no idea how I would make it through the Kol Nidre speech. I knew there would be at least five hundred people in the audience. I had no intention of revealing the newest bleak news. I had to hold on to this secret a bit longer, protect them a tiny bit longer, before I would terrify them all once again.

I thought about the meaning of Yom Kippur. During this most sacred of holidays, we are obligated to remember the sins we committed during the prior year and pray to God for forgiveness. God wipes the slate clean if you are truly repentant, and you begin anew, forgiven for your transgressions. Jews are obligated to fast for twenty-four hours as part of that penitence. I remembered all the transgressions I had committed, not just that year but in years past—disappointing my wife, shocking my children, family, and friends. They had all stood beside me, forgiven me. And then I got lung cancer. And now I had brain cancer, which would cause them all more pain.

I didn't know how I did it, but I got through the speech. When I was finished, I could see I had touched many in the audience. We were all vulnerable in this life we lived, some more obviously than others. But we were truly a community that offered love and strength to each other. My appreciation for the support I had been given was absolutely genuine, and when I said, "We greet this New Year with true optimism," I knew that many people wondered how I could be so positive. They didn't know I was wondering the same thing.

The next day, after we all returned from a full day of prayer and fasting in the synagogue and had eaten our "break-the-fast meal," I told my loved ones my news.

Of course, we all sat in the den. The familiar wooden shelving chock-full of albums filled with photos of our lives was eerily comforting but also equally foreboding. How many more years would I have to take the pictures that delighted me so?

"Dr. Stoopler called," I said. "My MRI revealed a tumor in my brain. I'm going to have to have surgery to remove the tumor, but he really thinks I should be all right."

They were silent, stunned. The words "brain tumor" had the same effect on them they'd had on me.

My mother got up and crossed the room. Barely five foot three inches tall, she walked straight and tall and sat down right next to me. She took my hand in hers. "Richard, it's going to be okay. You will be okay."

Once again, my mother showed the steel I needed, the grit that set the bar high, the example for everyone to follow. We would not despair. I held back my tears, both of gratitude and sorrow.

The worst part was disappointing and worrying everyone. It was not just me living with cancer. It was family and friends, and it was harder on them than on me. I owed it to them to make it as livable as possible.

I had the surgery successfully and was placed on chemotherapy immediately afterward. The surgery was awful, but not as bad as I'd feared. In fact, the chemotherapy was worse, but even that ended soon enough after several miserable months.

David nursed me through. He was not happy that I let him go to Arizona without telling him about the brain tumor, but he was strong. He refused to believe my cancer would kill me, or us.

Life Goes On...Thankfully

A Letter of Life

April 13, 2007
Dear Friends and Family,

Today is the third anniversary of my lung cancer diagnosis. It is truly a significant day, as I am now more than halfway to the lung cancer five-year survival milestone.

I was hoping this was going to be an uneventful health year, but as you know, I had a little run-in with a bump in my head last fall. I finished my four-month cycle of chemotherapy in February with my hair and optimism intact. I was thrilled to receive a clean brain MRI in February, CT scan in March, and PET scan in April.

My oncologist has decided to give me a break from chemotherapy (a lighter dose) "just to be sure." As I have said from the beginning, I will continue to do everything I am asked, if there is hope. And I continue to believe I have a chance to beat this terrible disease.

On a happy note, I accomplished one of my goals for 2007. I went skiing for the first time since my original diagnosis. Please know I was thinking of each of you as the chairlift dropped me at the top of Mont Tremblant in Montreal last month. I skied down the mountain with tears in my eyes but so thrilled that I could enjoy this experience again.

I know some of you might now be comparing these letters to the ones you receive during the holidays from distant relatives and acquaintances. But I continue to send this letter each year because as a cancer survivor, these are the moments we cherish, reflect [on], and strive to reach.

Please know how much I continue to appreciate each of you being on this journey with me. I am truly blessed to receive your hugs, love, cards, phone calls, emails, visits, encouragement, and support. Some gestures grand and some ordinary, but all generous in their own right. These are the things I will never forget.

There are so many special people in my life. Today, I want to mention my Mom and Dad for being with me every step of the way, Jodi for her unconditional love, Michael and Rachel for their inner strength and smiles, and David for only believing we will grow old together.

I look forward to celebrating my fourth and fifth (and many more) anniversaries with you.

Hope to see you on May 6th at the Murray Prawer Memorial Mitzvah Day Walk for the Lung Cancer Alliance.

Life goes on…thankfully.

Truly, all my love,

Richard

Twenty-One

The Picasso

Even as David cared for me, a bulwark against the unpredictable dangers of illness, I felt there was a part of him that was holding back, a part I couldn't reach. The trips and travel sometimes seemed like escape from our commitment, the shopping sprees suspiciously like diversions from a relationship was no longer as compelling as it once was. And worse, our sex life began to diminish. I felt his lack of passion, and I was deeply hurt. I loved his touch, his caress, the feel of his body next to mine.

"Come to bed," I'd urge late at night after a full workday and the inevitable dinners out and charitable events and Broadway shows.

"In a few minutes," he'd say, as if our sex life was no juicier than that of a fifties sitcom couple who slept in twin beds.

The minutes passed, silently trumpeting the unmistakable message that he had no desire to go to bed with me. Our relationship began to feel like a comfortable friendship, not a romance. I'd had decades of that with Jodi. I yearned for something more.

One day, a large package for David came to the apartment. It was a special delivery, preceded by several phone calls and requests for multiple personal signatures. I knew it was unusual and that the delivery was valuable.

When David got home, we opened it. It was an original Picasso.

I could not refrain from saying, "You bought a Picasso and you never even told me?"

"What's the problem? Now you know."

"I don't understand. Who buys a valuable painting like this without saying a word about it? This is a big deal. Am I that peripheral to your life that you didn't tell me about this?"

He looked weary. "Richard, I bought it. It's here. Why are you making such a fuss?"

Soon enough, there were more problems. I had been ill, after another setback, and was taking medicine that was making me nauseated. I'd just hung up with my friend Rebecca after a long and fun conversation, without telling her about my relapse or current distress.

He practically lunged at me. "Why can't you tell the truth when people ask you how you are feeling? You just went to the doctor and had two major procedures. You take medicine that makes you sick, and you never tell anyone. Why do you always have to put on a happy face for everyone?"

He was just getting warmed up. "Don't you realize that you're living in a dream world? You spend so much time taking care of your friends, sending those ridiculous birthday cards, and making sure you remember every detail of everyone's life. Why can't I be number one for a change?"

"Says the man who bought—"

"Actually, I don't even have to be number one, because I get that you have two kids, but how about number three? I'm not even that, because you always put your mother and Jodi first, not to mention your endless list of friends."

I was not a fighter.

Even as a child, I'd retreat from my brothers' teasing rather than fight back. Jodi came from a family of yellers. She'd pick a fight with me and then say, "Why aren't you yelling?"

Life Goes On...Thankfully

I considered it a wasted emotion. Yes, I allowed myself the feeling of frustration, but I could never stick with anger. Who was I going to get angry at? My boyfriend, who helped me through cancer? My mother, who might have to bury a child? My doctors, who did the best they could to keep me alive? My God, if he even exists? Why did I get cancer and face the risk that my children would grow up without a father?

"David," I said, "you are the one I love. You are the one who I go to bed with every night. You are the person I was always looking for. You have made this whole coming out worth it, and beyond that, I am probably not going to change all that much. You want me? You have me. With my obligations and my sense of humor and my *Playbill* collection and my one lung and my chest cavity full of breast implants, and my two children and my best little boy in the world syndrome."

Who said I was perfect?

We reconciled. We continued to live together, and one romantic evening, even though same-sex marriage was not yet legal in New York, David completely surprised me with a profound gesture of love. He bought two antique gold wedding rings, and he presented me with one, declaring his love for me.

"I'm clearly not perfect," he said. "I know I'm a real pain in the ass. But I do love you and want to be with you and share my life with you. And I want everyone to know you're mine."

I was ecstatic. I pushed aside any doubts and embraced our new, recommitted affair.

My life was fulfilling. I loved my work and my commitment to lung cancer advocacy. I put away thoughts of David's imperfections, knowing that life is short and mine could be shorter than most. I kept on traveling, kept on seeing the Broadway shows I adored. David became a fixture in our family.

During that time, I had several complications, culminating in a second brain tumor that had to be irradiated. Despite the fact that it was frightening, that tumor was more easily treated, and I was able to take this one more in stride. The procedure I required was called stereotactic radiosurgery, an exquisitely focused type of radiation. The brain tumor was zapped with a something called a gamma knife, which shot 192 beams of gamma rays that converged into one focal point and precisely targeted the lesion that needed to be eliminated. It minimized the damage to healthy brain tissue (and my raging anxiety). It was an outpatient procedure that I was told was quick and painless. I did not have to be admitted, but I did have to wear a large metallic crown on my head (think Statue of Liberty) that screamed *brain tumor*.

David was with me in the hospital when they attached that massive headpiece, literally screwing parts of it into my head. We had to go from one floor to another in an elevator crowded with staff, visitors, and patients, all looking straight ahead as people do in elevators, but I knew they were all looking at my crazy headpiece, worrying and feeling sorry for me.

But with David by my side, I felt brazen—or maybe it was the antianxiety medicine I had been given. Suddenly I began to moan, "Oh, my God, where am I? What's going to happen to me? Where am I going?" The people in the elevator were shocked, uncertain what to do. They didn't know that I just couldn't take the silent stares of pity, so I'd decided to lighten up the mood. David knew what I was doing, and I kept it up from the third floor to the twenty-third. Yes, it was crazy, but it made me feel better.

With David's ring on my finger and his stoic physical presence near, my future always seemed more possible, despite the uncertainty of how long that future might last.

My headpiece worked. I made it through that awful treatment and was "cured" of the brain tumor. Victory.

Life Goes On...Thankfully

A Letter of Life

April 12, 2008
Dear Friends and Family,

Today is the fourth anniversary of my lung cancer diagnosis. It is truly a significant day, as I am now within one year of reaching the lung cancer five-year survival milestone.

I was hoping this was going to be a boring health year, but as you know, I had tumors successfully removed from my chest in June and my brain in December. I was relieved and thrilled to receive clean brain MRI and CT scan reports last month.

I recently read an article in the *New York Times* titled, "When the Body Decides to Stop Following the Rules." The author, Loren Berlin, wrote that a college professor provided her with a definition of fate.

"Describing an ancient Greek perspective, he explained that fate can be imagined as a plot of fenced land. The individual cannot control where the fence stakes are placed. But every person determines for themselves how they will maneuver within the enclosed space."

These past four years, I have spoken a lot about hope and believing that things will work out even if I don't know how. Living with lung cancer is my fence hammered into the ground at an unfortunate angle. I have accepted the countless things beyond my control, but how I live my life with lung cancer is my decision. And live, I will.

I know that in one form or another, my life will continue, and it will include my dear friends, magnificent family, particularly my brothers, parents, Jodi, Michael, Rachel and especially David for his benevolence, unconditional love, and always seeing me as healthy.

Please know how much I continue to appreciate each of you standing by the symbolic fence of my life. I am very thankful for your cards, phone calls, emails, and time together. I will never forget your acts of kindness, thoughtfulness, encouragement, and love.

I look forward to celebrating my fifth (and many more) anniversaries with you.

Life goes on…thankfully.

Truly, all my love,
Richard

Twenty-Two

Life, Death, and Boredom

> Your life is a sham
> Till you can shout out,
> "I am what I am."
> ~A lyric from "I Am What I Am" in *La Cage Aux Folles*

David and I were rarely still and always planning the next trip. He spent money like water and loved not only me, but my children. It made the cancer drumbeat just background noise. Even though we occasionally were forced to focus on the fact of my illness, I felt as though I really was beating cancer, with the added benefit of living vibrantly and enjoying every day to its fullest.

My life was practically as thrilling as the shows I continued to attend and cherish. I was surrounded by loyal friends and family who loved me.

I often joked that cancer had given me a get-out-of-jail-free card. Anyone who thought I had betrayed my loved ones by coming out and changing my life so dramatically gave me a pass because of my illness. Right or wrong, sick or healthy, straight or gay, I tried to live each day to its fullest.

~

The following year, in November 2008, I was diagnosed with multiple small tumors on my left lung. I immediately began chemotherapy.

Those who have had the otherworldly experience of receiving chemotherapy in a hospital will understand the odd juxtaposition of life-and-death matters and stultifying boredom. Perhaps prisoners understand it, or soldiers marking time before uncertain battle, or victims of long wars who suffer mind-numbing occupations in the killing fields by their oppressors. The survival instinct meets the doldrums of endless routine in a cancer hospital, where patients go to receive the lifeblood that is their chemo.

I spent many hours in a big La-Z-Boy-type chair with my arm extended and vein pierced to accept the chemotherapy that would save my life. I was forced to understand that my life was just one among many in the room filled with patients who suffered the same fate that I did. But I chose not to despair.

> Things you think about when your arm is attached to a poisonous drug that will kill your cancer and hopefully save your life:
> 1) Am I really here? or Why me?
> 2) The people who are surprisingly nice to you.
> 3) The people who are surprisingly mean to you.
> 4) The people who are most important to you.
> 5) The traffic to get to the hospital.
> 6) The traffic to get home from the hospital.
> 7) Let's get this over with.

The irony of it all, for those of us who have resolved to live in the moment, is that chemo days are incredibly boring. A friend donated a television and DVD player to the hospital so the patients who had to sit for hours on end would be entertained. I donated the film, *Hello, Dolly*, which I'd always loved. I saw the movie countless times, and the show four times on Broadway. I loved the score. The music always made me happy. The entire script was so satisfyingly predictable. The plot was always engaging. There were no ugly surprises, only a happy ending, and I always loved a happy ending. And, of course, we didn't know how this was going to end.

I helped build a library of movies and television shows to help patients in that room pass the time, to provide a distraction from nausea or fear, and to create just a small boost to make the long hours pass more engagingly. And for those who could lose themselves and their worries in the movies, that was no small victory in the daily battle with a deadly enemy.

A Letter of Life

April 13, 2009
Dear Friends and Family,

Today is the fifth anniversary of my lung cancer diagnosis. This year it is an emotional and statistical day of reflection for me.

I consider every day a special gift because, of the approximately one million people diagnosed with lung cancer since April 13, 2004, more than eight hundred thousand have lost their lives to this disease.

Five years ago, I had no idea where this journey was going to take me. There were many times I just assumed I would be cured of cancer because it was detected early. But the last six months have been my most serious dose of reality. I now know more than ever that my lung cancer is relentless, tenacious, and unpredictable.

Since November, I have been in chemotherapy when new tumors were detected on my left lung. The good news is the most recent CT scan in March showed no new tumors, some tumors decreasing in size, and the largest tumor dying. I will continue in chemotherapy for an indefinite period of time.

I will always worry about the next reoccurrence. But I know I can live with reoccurrences if it means I have a chance to beat cancer for a period of time and enjoy my life. And hopefully if there is another reoccurrence, there will be new treatments available to keep me alive longer.

I wish I could say confidently [that] I believe things will work out well just because they will. But that might not be true. I do not want to die but have accepted the fact it is a possibility and there is only

Life Goes On...Thankfully

so much I can do about it. But fight, *I will.* I will continue to do everything my doctors recommend to me.

So even though I now live with the uncertainty of the future, I know a few things are in my power. I have a phenomenal partner, close family, terrific children, many caring friends, wonderful memories, and more dreams to attain in the time ahead. This is all I really need.

Please do not think of the last five years as "sick years" for me. Even though my life does not always look easy, it is still good. My life is worth living, no matter how difficult the course. I am going to continue to make the most of everything that comes along my way.

If there is one lesson to learn from my journey, it is never to take life's special moments for granted. Time waits for no one. Treasure every moment you have. My next moment is Michael's graduation from the University of Wisconsin in May. I am counting the days till I am in Madison with David, Jodi, Rachel, Grandpa Arnold, Grandma Audrey, and Grandma Max, cheering for Michael as he receives his college diploma.

Today, I toast my doctors for keeping me alive and giving me the opportunity to have a good quality of life. I continue to have unconditional faith in my team of doctors at Columbia Presbyterian. I have thankfully put my life in the hands of Dr. Roger Maxfield, Dr. Joshua Sonett and Dr. Mark Stoopler. I truly appreciate all their time, concern, and expertise.

So now my fight continues toward my *sixth anniversary* and beyond. And as I have said for years, I am so thankful to everyone for your phone calls, text messages, emails, cards, hugs, and visits. Your love and support are truly as important as any of my treatments. Too often we underestimate the power of a smile, a kind word, a listening ear, a compliment, or the smallest act of caring, all of which have made my days and life so much better.

Life goes on...thankfully.
Love,
Richard

Twenty-Three

Betrayal

Perhaps the constant threat of illness made me insatiable. I desperately wanted a full life, and I wanted that life to include a fulfilling sexual relationship. I had waited so long and gone through so much to find my true sexual being. I wanted a man to climb into bed with at night and feel the weight of his body on me, his hands caressing every part of me, and his ardor easily aroused. I had to admit to myself that David and I, so compatible in so many ways, were not sexually compatible. He was happy with little or no sex. I craved more intimacy. I felt we were little more than great friends. The distance between us seemed to hang in the air from the cushions of the antique sofa to the glittering chandeliers.

Then, betrayal.

David stopped coming home from work as usual. He began to be absent at odd times. I became suspicious and then jealous. Finally, I could not control my impulse to stalk him. I went to his office building to see if he would leave at his usual time. I stood on a corner, lurking like a tawdry private eye in a B movie with a baseball cap I'd bought on the street pulled low over my face. I knew I was humiliating myself, but I couldn't help it.

Soon enough, David came out. I followed him toward a nearby hotel, famed for its glittering bar scene. I kept a close pace so I wouldn't lose him, glad the streets were crowded with rush-hour pedestrians. I literally slipped into the revolving door of the hotel just a few revolutions after he did, dawdled in the reception area for a few minutes, and then walked into the lobby bar, where I saw him sitting on a banquette leaning intimately toward a man I immediately recognized as one of his old lovers.

I stood out of sight and had a clear view of them flirting with each other at the table. I had no heart for either confrontation or reconciliation. If he could buy a Picasso without telling me or have sex with another man while professing great love for me, what was the point?

~

It took me only three days to find a new apartment. I said absolutely nothing in the meantime, pretending that everything was the same. I steamed about our upcoming confrontation and his betrayal, but I knew that no matter what words were exchanged between us, I was leaving. I carried a leaden weight in the pit of my stomach, a toxic mix of anger and jealousy and sadness.

The morning of my move, I confronted him in the kitchen where he had so generously cooked for Michael.

"I'm moving out today, right now. I know you're cheating on me. There's nothing more to say, David." I was breathing heavily, and I could barely look him in the eye, but I got the words out.

I wanted him to beg me to stay so I could refuse, but he didn't. I was disappointed that he didn't argue or look the least bit surprised. Instead, he simply looked at me with a pained expression on his face and drew a breath. "I'm tired of being your sycophant, Richard. I need someone who needs me. You don't. You've got way too many people in your life. Between your family and your friends, it's clear that I always come in last."

In a way, he was right. I could never make a choice about who I loved the most in my life. To be asked to do so was abusive, and I wanted no part of it.

Alone in my new, bare apartment, I began to unravel. My usual coping mechanisms—family, friends, theater, travel, work—all failed me. One day, I awoke feeling particularly despondent. I could not bring myself to face the day ahead. I cancelled the appointments I had and drove to see my mother in Connecticut. She took me out to lunch, hoping to cheer me up. Just being in her strong, reliable presence made it possible for me to let my guard down.

"Something is terribly wrong," I said. "I think I need to go to a hospital."

She eyed me with concern. "What do you mean?"

"I...don't...know. I just feel like I'd be better off with...well, with someone watching me." I could not stop the tears that gathered in my eyes and fell down my cheeks. "I feel terrible. I can't eat, I can't sleep, and I can't stop these dreadful thoughts that I'd be better off dead."

It was the first time I recognized the misery that was washing over me. Not even trusting myself to stay at home in my barren apartment all alone, I slept that night in my parents' house. As usual, my mother filled my father in on my condition, and later that evening, he knocked on the door of the bedroom. He was stiff, but he said, "Richard, we are going to get you some help. You'll be okay." I knew he was trying to help, but I was so miserable, his words fell on deaf ears.

The next day, they took me to see Dr. Stoopler, the surgeon from Columbia-Presbyterian Hospital who had saved me several times over already. Dr. Stoopler usually kept me waiting for hours in his crowded waiting room, so busy was he with his great crop of cancer patients and his old-fashioned way of delivering quality care accompanied by a kind, unhurried, bedside manner. This time, I was ushered into his office, not an examination room, almost immediately.

I sat across from him with a deeply uncomfortable mix of despair and shame. I always tried to put my best self forward with Dr. Stoopler, because, of course, I wanted to be his favorite patient.

Unlike many unfortunate victims of lung cancer, I understood my illness and could converse on the complexities of many of the issues facing lung cancer patients. I was able to make intelligent decisions with him as my doctor and my advocate. I did not want to be just another miserable soul in his practice.

Well, so much for that.

He looked at me intently with his kind, perceptive eyes, leaning in toward me as he spoke. "Richard, can you tell me how you're feeling? What's going on?"

In his comfortable, reassuring presence, I gave voice to my fears for the first time. "I've come all this way, but I can't seem to make my life work...I can't find love...I can't find a purpose...I can't eat. I can't sleep. I'm not myself. I can't see a reason to get better when I'll only get worse again."

"Are you having thoughts of taking your own life, Richard?"

I admitted that I was, although I had no clear plan. But the future looked nightmarish where once it had been so bright, and I could find no solace in the space around me.

"Okay, I'm making an appointment for you with a psychiatrist for today. Don't leave the office until I get it set up; understand?"

He sent me to a man he respected named Robert Berman, who he thought would understand my issues and help me get back on track. My parents took me to his office, greeted him with me, and then left me to speak with him. They sat in his waiting room until he could give them an evaluation.

I liked Dr. Berman as soon as I saw him, even though I was feeling so low. He was about ten years older than I was, and he was very well dressed—bow tie, an oxford shirt, and rimless glasses on an unlined face. His office looked like the quintessential Upper East Side shrink's office, with walls lined with bookcases filled with medical books. Some were lined up neatly in a row, but many were askew and worn, showing they had actually been read. There was a large desk loaded with papers and medical journals. Two big, comfortable chairs sat prominently across from each other, and a sofa occupied one side of the room.

I sat nervously in one of the big chairs across from him during our initial interview, during which he decided if I had to be hospitalized as a suicide risk. He asked me the usual questions a shrink asks to see if someone is thinking of suicide or is in the throes of a major depressive episode.

No, I was not sleeping well.

Yes, I got up earlier than usual in the morning, about 4:00 a.m.

Yes, I felt a little better at the end of the day than I did when I got up.

No, I had no appetite.

Yes, I had lost weight.

Yes, I had broken up with my significant other and felt despondent over it.

No, I had no plans to hurt myself, nor the thought to do so, but I did feel hopeless and wondered if I'd be better off dead instead of dragging out this terrible situation that would just hurt my loved ones.

I sat with my ankles crossed and my hands on my knees, wiping my khaki pants. My throat was dry, and my voice hesitant. I cried as we spoke, but I liked his kind voice, the sensitive way he asked questions. I began to feel he might be able to help me. I told him I was feeling overwhelmed with grief, that I had lost David and my hopes for a life filled with reciprocal love. I also told him that my mother's brother was bipolar and had committed suicide, and I would never subject my mother to that again.

"Richard, I don't think you need hospitalization as long as you stay with your parents for a while. I don't want you to be alone. I'm going to give you a tranquilizer to help you sleep and start you on an antidepressant. We'll meet every day this week and then determine a new schedule for you depending on how you're feeling. I believe you're suffering from depression, and I don't know how long it will last, but most depressions do lift, and since you've never been depressed before, I think you have a good prognosis."

I saw Dr. Berman for a year.

Life Goes On...Thankfully

Our first sessions were short. I was hardly able to talk. It felt as though my mind was encased in a shroud. Every answer I gave was slow and labored. My tongue felt thick, and my brain, sluggish. Dr. Berman asked mainly about my physical health. Was I sleeping, eating, moving my bowels, short of breath? He also asked about my mood, which was dark, and he always asked if I was still feeling as if I would be better off dead or if I had any thoughts of hurting myself.

I sat in his office, upright and anxious, with my right leg jiggling seemingly on its own, and answered all his questions as honestly as I could.

Mainly, I suffered from thoughts that I had destroyed my family, disappointed my parents, and was being punished with cancer. The thoughts were like daggers, stabbing me over and over. It was the darkest period I had ever endured. I had no control, and it went on without respite. I lost a lot of weight and had to let my family take care of me. They all took turns, either taking me to the psychiatrist or the medical doctors who were following up on my cancer care. I was a full-time job for everyone, and there was nothing I could do about it.

Dr. Berman's first challenge was to find the right antidepressants for me, which, given the other meds I was on, required a fair amount of pharmacological expertise. I was lucky. The drugs he suggested eventually began to work.

Gradually, my mood started to lift. I was able to speak with more animation and energy, increasingly free from the frozen, dark, joyless morass in which I had been buried.

Once I could actually talk, Dr. Berman zeroed in on the beginning. "Can you tell me about your father?" he asked.

I told him about an incident, tears welling in my eyes as I spoke, that I had not thought about for a very long time. I wasn't sure why it came to me at that moment, but the pain I felt as I told the story felt devastating.

"When I was just a little boy, perhaps four or five years old, I loved watching *Bewitched* and *I Love Lucy*. In fact, I chattered about those shows a lot, looked forward to them, and made elaborate plans to watch television with my favorite blanket and snack. I loved hunkering down in the corner of our sectional sofa in the living room and getting lost in my private reveries as I watched. I usually watched alone, because my brothers were completely disinterested, preferring to play Ping-Pong in the basement.

"One night, my father came into the room while I was watching.

"'Get up!' he shouted. 'You watch the same damned shows over and over again. Get out of here and go play Ping-Pong with your brothers!'

"I was caught completely off guard and started crying.

"Then my mother came in. She looked like she was ready to kill him. 'What are you doing, Arnold? Leave him alone! He's not bothering anybody…Let him watch his shows, for crying out loud!'

"I looked helplessly from one to the other. My father's angry words felt like blows. He didn't see the amusement or happiness in the shows that I did, and something about my enchantment upset him. He wanted to forcefully yank me away from doing what I loved. He wanted me to be like my brothers and play their stupid games, and I knew at that moment that I was going to have to hide a part of myself if I wanted him to love me. I felt so ashamed, and I wondered if he loved me at all."

"Your mother protected you?" Dr. Berman asked.

"She was my guardian angel. She understood me and loved me with no conditions. We had a connection that was unspoken. I knew that under the umbrella of my mother's love, I was safe."

Those sessions in Dr. Berman's office helped me understand that I was not so very different from a lot of gay men. He helped me see that in my earliest cognitive moments, I felt a deep sense of shame—a feeling that somehow I was "off." I was petrified that my father would sense that I was different and hate me for it. My mother somehow perceived it as well, and, whether she was aware of it or not, swooped in to try to protect me.

Life Goes On...Thankfully

I realized that I created a divide between them, and that they disagreed over the best way to handle the "problem" I presented. Should I be left alone to be myself or pressured to be more like my brothers? All of this was unspoken, but still it formed a vital undercurrent in all of our lives. It was the genesis of my desire to be the best little boy in the world, one who had an insatiable desire for love and acceptance, while fearing all the while that there was something about me that made me essentially unlovable.

I understood that as I grew up, I adopted compensating behaviors that were sure to make me lovable. I loved to make people laugh. I had a sense of humor that was both quick and occasionally wicked. Everyone adored me for it.

But I was also sympathetic, generous, and kind and went out of my way to extend myself to my friends. If someone I knew was in the hospital, I always went to visit, and I knew those visits were appreciated. I even visited sick congregants from our synagogue when I knew it was the rabbi's job. My mother had taught me that if something important or difficult needs to be done, one should step up and do it, not look around for someone else to do it. Of course, as David had said, sometimes I overdid it, even attending two events in the same day when they were far apart and involved hours in a car.

People came to expect these things of me, and I never considered it a burden. I wanted to be counted on to be at celebrations and funerals—all events of importance, no matter how far away the locale. All of these things made me beloved and cherished. This unconscious drive to please others was a fundamental part of who I was.

I sought validation in the traditional Jewish life and clung to it desperately in the hope that I would not have to face my sexuality. Married, father of two, a huge social circle, president of the temple, a beautiful house in the suburbs, travel and nice cars, financial freedom, a position of prominence in the community—shouldn't that have been enough to cover up my shame?

Apparently not.

I was cunning in the way I garnered love, friendship, envy, and popularity from the people I knew. Hiding my identity was primal. I could not imagine living any other way. Until it all broke down and I faced my truest self.

And what of the men I loved? Were they any different? Did they not face the same battles I did? Was my love affair with handsome Robert doomed from the start? He wasn't capable of any kind of long-term love, even though he was capable of kindness as well as cruelty. He was not able to stay true to one man, and I wanted a single, dedicated love, an overwhelming love, like I had dreamed of my whole life. David, too, with his expensive antiques, his enviable New York apartment, and his exotic travel, was another gay man who sought validation in glitter and glamour, and his relationship with me was challenged by my very honest wish that he love me and me alone and trust that I could love him back.

Even after I was diagnosed with cancer, I still wanted to live the life I had dreamed of for myself. I craved one true love; I yearned to see my children get married; I dreamed of the joy of seeing their babies and being a grandfather. I desperately hoped to outlive my mother to spare her the agony of my death. I wanted to continue to share the lives of my friends and help others with the battle against cancer. I wanted to continue the all-important business of making memories with the people I love. And most importantly, I did not want to be a cancer victim or a victim of any kind, in anyone's eyes.

During this black time in my life, I lost the ability to believe in my dreams. I, the consummate planner, mourned that I could no longer engage in carefree talk of the future. I couldn't say with certainty, "I'll be a grandfather one day" or "for my next car lease, I'm going to get a Volvo." That kind of talk was for people who were healthy, who didn't worry that something would interfere with their plans. I had to come to terms with living in the present, without a guarantee, and making the most of what I had each day.

Life Goes On...Thankfully

All of that felt impossible to me, but as I felt better, I started to believe in myself again. My perspective shifted, my mood had lifted, and I was strong enough to start fighting again for my life.

I began to learn how to live in the present. It took a lot of redirecting.

Most of us assume we'll grow old. I had to accept that my script was already written, and I was the character who was leaving the show while the other characters lived on. I was going to be the character about whom fans would say, "I can't believe they killed him off." I had to appreciate a good long life for what it was—a privilege, not a right.

I tried hard to be thankful for all that I had and to live without bitterness. Of course, I feared I would not be present for the moments I had always imagined—the weddings, the grandchildren, the vacations, the family celebrations of holidays. I taught myself to think about the moments I did have, not the ones I would not have. Yes, I wanted to be present for those I loved for as long as I could and continue to make memories for them all. I loved being a vital part of life, and I resolved to continue no matter what.

A woman I became friendly with at a cancer board meeting—I think she wanted to date me until she found out I was not eligible—had been diagnosed with small-cell lung cancer, an even more menacing diagnosis than mine. She had a house on the beach in East Hampton, Long Island, and she told me she was hoping for one more summer in the Hamptons. I understood. I thought the same way.

I wanted one more of whatever it was, too. That was how I lived with cancer.

Twenty-Four

Would You Rather?

Sometimes I played a game with myself. When I saw someone without a leg, or someone with a deformity, or heard of a person with Alzheimer's, I asked myself, "Would I trade places with that person?" Losing a lung is a really big deal. If I had to be disabled, would I rather go through life without one arm? Would that be better? Easier?

Was I bitter when I said it's not sad when a person dies at ninety-two? Yes, that person was gone. But he got to live a lot longer than me. I know it made me sound cold, but those thoughts did occur to me. I couldn't help it.

Would I trade places with the guys working in the underground garage at Memorial Sloan Kettering Cancer Center, parking the cars of the patients and their families? They knew everyone there was dealing with terrifying illness, skirting the edge of life and death. They were kind every time they brought my car around for me. They worked all day in the dark, underground garage. Would I trade my fate for theirs?

I finished my treatment with Dr. Berman after one year. He told me that he had learned as much from me as I had from him, making me feel like I was a special patient. Of course that gratified my ego—what patient doesn't want to feel like he's memorable to his shrink? But we agreed I was better. I was continuing my work

Life Goes On...Thankfully

for the Lung Cancer Alliance and the synagogue in New Jersey, and I was back to spending time with friends and family.

One day, I learned that Roy, one of David's ninety-year-old uncles, was in the hospital. I had an independent, joyful relationship with both of David's uncles even after David and I broke up, so I went to visit the uncle in the hospital. To no one's surprise, David was there. I hadn't seen or spoken to him for a year. I knew immediately the old anger was gone. I was so happy to see him that I could not stop my heart from racing.

He seemed thrilled to see me, too. We talked as if we had not endured a betrayal, a year's separation, or any of the disappointments of our relationship. I put my hand on his knee, and I said, "I don't think I can keep my hands off you."

He welcomed me back, and it was as if we were on a second honeymoon. The trips began again. We went as far as Australia, visiting the Sydney Opera House and the Great Barrier Reef. My family accepted David all over again. The cancer drumbeat was reduced to background noise. Even though occasionally we were forced to focus on the fact of my illness, I felt like I really *was* beating cancer, with the added benefit of living vibrantly and enjoying every day to its fullest.

One of my favorite teachings in Judaism is the concept that we are all responsible for our fellow man and blessed by God when we reach out in any way, large or small, to help another. I accepted as a personal responsibility the idea that if someone needs you, you should help them, even if it is inconvenient or troublesome. Or, as my mother taught me, when you see something that needs doing, don't talk about it; just do it.

My good friend Phyllis, a woman in her sixties, was a former buyer from the days of the costume-jewelry business. She was diagnosed with bladder cancer and was embarrassed because the illness forced her to wear a bag to hold her urine.

I went to visit her every morning while she was in the hospital. I know full well that in the immediate postoperative period, you look awful. In addition to the often-catastrophic blow your health has sustained, you look pale and worn. Hospital gowns are rarely flattering. And you can't avoid the truth by ignoring mirrors, because you know you look as bad as all those other patients you see trudging down the hallway, pushing an IV pole, with their hospital gowns occasionally swinging open to reveal their assets to the world. Visitors are the most critical reminder that you are important and loved and a part of life.

After her surgery, my dear old friend Phyllis was miserable, but she grinned widely when she saw me.

"Love your new bag, Phyllis," I said when I entered her hospital room. "But you've got to stop buying such expensive accessories and go back to the cheap knockoffs we love so much."

"Oh, shut up and give me that bagel and coffee you brought me. The coffee will just make me fill up the bag quicker and give the poor nurses more work to do."

We reminisced about the time I took her out for dinner and took her home, right to the door of her apartment on the fifteenth floor of a high-rise. I had been taught that when I took a woman out, it was my responsibility to deliver her right to her door and be certain she was safely inside before I left. As we went up in her elevator that evening, another man was in the car with us. He looked at us, trying to figure out our relationship.

I said, "You know what's going to happen up there, right? I'm totally enamored of this woman."

Phyllis was so embarrassed that she sputtered, "He's my nephew; don't listen to him!"

After that, every time the man saw her in the building, he'd ask, "How's your nephew?"

A Letter of Life

August 30, 2010
Dear Friends and Family,

As many of you know, for the last six weeks, I have been on a clinical trial for a new lung cancer drug manufactured by Pfizer.

Today I had my first scan since beginning the trial, and I am thrilled to tell you that my two largest tumors have cavitated (that is medical jargon for *died*). These tumors were detected two years ago, and they are finally, no longer active.

I still have several very small tumors on my lung, but they continue to be stable. I will be on the clinical trial for the foreseeable future.

This is a good day on the emotional roller coaster ride I have been on for over six years. I celebrate the news from today with you, but I also understand that there are no guarantees the clinical trial drug will work forever.

Gilda Radner wrote, "I've learned, the hard way, that some poems don't rhyme, and some stories don't have a clear beginning, middle, and end. Life is about not knowing, having to change, taking the moment and making the best of it without knowing what's going to happen next."

Since being diagnosed, I have learned a lot about living and aging. I now know that aging is a privilege, and many people do not get that privilege. But I am an optimist, and even though I do not know what tomorrow will bring, I will continue to think and dream about my future.

Today is one of those "moments" for all of us to enjoy and savor. Thank you again for your love and support.

Life goes on…thankfully,
Richard

Bonnie Adler

A Letter of Life

April 13, 2011
Dear Friends and Family,

    I vacillated this year about sending a letter, since it was not a "5" or "0" anniversary of my diagnosis, but it is the **seventh year** since that fateful day, and I felt it was a good time for me to exhale a bit.

    I am thrilled to say that I am now starting my fourteenth cycle (each cycle is three weeks) of my clinical trial with Pfizer. My tumors have disappeared or are stable, my pulmonary function numbers are the best in years, and my doctors are thrilled with the results.

    But this year especially showed me up close the fragility of life, as one of my lung cancer phone buddies and two dear friends' fathers passed away from lung-related cancer.

    I never thought about dying from lung cancer when I was diagnosed, probably because I was so naïve about the survival facts. But I did believe "that my life will be less long," as Elizabeth Edwards said. And even though my life might not be measured by the number of breaths I take but by the number of moments that take my breath away like celebrating Rachel's twenty-first birthday this year via cyberspace between New York and Tel Aviv or hiking through caves in Belize with David, Michael, and Rachel.

    Martin Luther King Jr. said, "You don't have to see the whole staircase. Just take the first step." Over the last seven years, I sometimes felt like I was taking one step forward and two steps back, but I've learned that what is important is making that one step count.

    I know cancer has helped to shape my life, and it has settled into the fiber of my being. For everything lung cancer has taken, something with greater value has been given. Cancer came into my life, and I could not stop it, but there are things cancer cannot do. It cannot end my happiness, cannot cripple my love, shatter my hope, kill my friendships, or suppress my memories.

I dedicate today to some of the people who do not know they make a difference in my life. One such person is the woman at my local delicatessen where I pick up my breakfast on the days when I have my scans, who thoughtfully puts my food and beverages into my cooler; my lung cancer pen pal, who is in prison (yes, prison), who wrote, "You give me hope and strength to carry on with this fight"; my oncology nurse, Denisa, whose instinctive decision to resubmit my tumor tissue sample for acceptance into the clinical trial after the first sample had been rejected might have saved my life; and Carol at the New York Yankees, who, last year, gave me play-off game tickets for Michael and me on the day I found out my tumors had grown slightly.

And to all of you who also make a difference in my life every minute, every hour, and every day, I thank you so much for continuing on this journey with me. I cannot imagine my life without each of you. I am so fortunate to have you in my life.

The word "impossible" became very prominent in my vocabulary and life seven years ago today. One of the lessons I have learned is nothing is impossible. There is no doubt that I am going to get the most out of every day of my life. And I know what I am going to continue to do and that is to live, love, laugh, and dare the impossible until I no longer can.

Life goes on...thankfully,
Richard

Bonnie Adler

A Letter of Life

April 13, 2012
Dear Friends and Family,

Today is my eighth anniversary since being diagnosed with cancer and my 636th precious day in Pfizer's clinical trial for Xalkori.

Thankfully, my oncologist and pulmonologist cannot see any tumors on the CT scans. My pulmonary function is the best in eight years. I feel great. Most importantly, my doctors are using the word "remission" for the first time in three years.

Lung cancer is no longer a "death or cure" disease. Now it can also be chronic and livable. Living with cancer is a very different way to live, but I now know it can be very beautiful, enjoyable, and satisfying.

I recently read "the two most important days in a person's life are the day you were born and the day you discover why you were born." I now believe one of the reasons I was born is to be a voice for the approximately 1,440,000 people who have died of lung cancer since I was diagnosed in 2004. Sadly, these people can no longer share their stories with others. This year, I had the opportunity to tell my story at an international patient advocate organization's conference, to Pfizer's worldwide employees at their quarterly meeting, and in Washington, DC, on behalf of a bill for Advanced Diagnostics: Getting the Right Treatments to the Right People.

I dedicate this anniversary to my two most significant caregivers, my mother and David.

My mother has worn many hats over the past eight years, as my relentless advocate, consistent caregiver, and loving mom. I hope

Life Goes On...Thankfully

never to understand how difficult it was for my mother and father to hear their healthy son was diagnosed with lung cancer. My mother said many times if she could change places with me, she would. And I know she would if she could. I do not think I would be alive today without my mother's love and support.

I met David almost six years ago, and we have lived a lifetime of love, loss, sadness, and happiness since July 31, 2006. David has been at my side for all five of my reoccurrences and too many trips to the emergency room. He continues to cheer me on every day and only sees me as a healthy person. I know in David's heart, the cup is overflowing with love, devotion, and optimism for many happy times together in the years ahead.

I am thrilled as my next two wish-list moments are within my sight: Rachel's Penn State graduation in May and my mom's 80th birthday in June. I am sure eight years ago my doctors would never have predicted I would be alive to witness these two wonderful moments.

And to all of you who also make a difference in my life, especially Michael and Rachel, thank you for giving me the strength, courage, and determination to continue to fight for every new day. I could not imagine this surreal journey without you.

I know life has only a finite number of heartbeats, so in honor of my eighth anniversary, I encourage you to have dessert tonight, as life is too short to refuse anything good.

On a serious note, I ask you to pray for David's father, Jerry, as he continues to fight his own courageous battle with lung cancer. Since the day I met him, he has been an inspiration to me for his tenacity, hope, and unwavering faith.

Finally, as the American Cancer Society motto states, I look forward to "a world with less cancer and more birthdays."

Life goes on...thankfully.

Love,

Richard

Twenty-Five

One More Key Exchange

Although David and I reconciled, we could not make the relationship endure, no matter how much we both wanted to. We had flash and humor when we were with our friends and even our families, but alone, we were critical and nitpicky with each other.

I knew David was unhappy, but I had no idea how to fix things. Despite the identical rings we wore on our ring fingers, David did not want to get married. He thought he was independent. I thought he was emotionally unavailable and secretive. He thought I craved love and adoration from others to a ridiculous extent.

One day, I saw a large, thick envelope on his desk from a real estate firm in Arizona. It was addressed to him. It looked like it held legal documents and was marked "Private and Confidential." I decided to open the envelope. And there it was—a document that confirmed the purchase of a house in Arizona. The owner of record, to my disbelieving eyes, was David.

He had done it again. First, it was an expensive Picasso, a treasure he purchased with no word to me. This time, he'd bought an expensive property in Arizona without telling me anything about it. Was it a getaway, a place to find refuge away from me? I was stunned and hurt, and I understood with bruising finality that some things would never change. I wanted a relationship with no secrets, no bizarre surprises that would indicate my lover and soul mate did not trust me. This was too far a cry from the loving, open relationship I coveted.

Once again, I found myself in the painful position of ending the relationship. We sat in the living room, in front of the television, and I spit out the words that I could not contain.

"I'm leaving you," I said.

I watched his face for a reaction. There was absolutely none, except for a clenched jaw. "Really?" he said, stone faced and angry. He changed the channel on the television, acting as if I had not uttered those words, his eyes glued to the screen.

"Aren't you even going to ask me why?" I said. My heart was thudding, my breath uneven. I was sickened and incredulous.

"Why should I? You have obviously made up your mind. So go."

We sat in silence. I did not feel like unwinding my words. I did not wish to retrieve them. I looked at his face, his stiffened back, and his angry mouth. I knew it was irretrievably, irrevocably over.

"You know, Richard," he said, finally turning toward me, "I can't believe that you are leaving now, just when you are feeling well again. You are really selfish. I've stood right by your side, helping you while you've been sick, and now, when you are in complete remission, you're leaving me?"

I couldn't believe his words. He bought a secret ranch in another state thousands of miles away, one which I knew he had no interest in revealing to me, and he resented me for leaving when I was strong. The chasm between us was so vast that I knew we were lost. There was no hope of reconciliation.

After our split, alone in my own apartment, I told myself that if I had to live my life as a single man, I would enjoy it. I would have my children, my brothers, my parents, our extended family, and all my friends, and I would be just fine. I threw my renewed energy back into my advocacy. I worked even harder with my colleagues at the Lung Cancer Alliance and accepted even more of the offers to speak that came my way.

I had become an excellent public speaker, which was a bit of a surprise to me, because I had always had such terrible stage fright when I was younger and dreamed of being an actor.

One of my most memorable speeches was at a Pfizer meeting in the Midwest, where I met with a large research team. I knew very well that the people in the audience worked in labs, hunkered over tiny test tubes and microscopes, to create the next experimental drug. Since I had been the beneficiary of their miracles, I wanted to share the impact of illness with them all. I wanted them to know the value of their work.

I used humor, hope, and pathos to my advantage. My words carried weight because I was a victim and could express myself eloquently. I spoke from my heart. When I expressed hope for miraculous cures on the horizon, I was speaking for all victims of lung cancer.

"Thank you," I said, "from the bottom of my one lung." That always drew a laugh. "You have given me the hope that someday I will dance at my daughter's wedding." That always drew a tear.

With the Lung Cancer Alliance as my "team" and the drug companies as my public relations agents, I was able to reach thousands of people who had an interest in helping to raise money and awareness for my cause. I became the face of lung cancer for people who could not speak for themselves, and despite the fact that I had to publicly embrace a cancer diagnosis, I felt that speaking out was not only worthwhile but crucial. I was good at it. I knew how to reach people to help the great cause of finding more money to cure the disease and to reduce its terrible stigma.

For cancer patients who did not respond to standard treatments, there was always the hope that research and participation in a clinical trial of experimental drugs could work. Medicines that were brand new and risky helped some and not others, but those who could benefit lived longer because of their participation in these trials. Above all, the new drugs created hope, and hope was the most important thing for victims, their families, and their medical teams.

I believed there was a void of hope among those living with lung cancer. After all, victims are often one telephone call away from a worsening scenario. But when I spoke of hope, I was at my best, for I was by nature an optimist.

I had become a hot ticket on the cancer circuit. I accepted the responsibility and spoke when invited and as needed, and of course, health permitting.

One of the most exciting moments was the day I rang the bell at the New York Stock Exchange in the name of a cure for lung cancer. I was not an actor, but I was on a world stage, and I was thrilled to accept the role, because it was in the name of hope. That day, I met a woman who had lived with lung cancer for twelve years, a real record. I wanted her right up front when we rang the bell, for it was she who provided hope for us all.

A Letter of Life

April 13, 2013
Dear Friends and Family,

Today is my ninth anniversary since being diagnosed with cancer and my 1,000th unfathomable day on Pfizer's gene-targeted therapy drug, Xalkori.

I am sure in the spring of 2004 my doctors would never have predicted I would be alive today. It is very daunting to look back and realize I continue to beat the odds. I have accepted the truth about my illness. I know every day is a gift, because I almost had every day taken away from me.

I also never thought, why me? I think, it's life. And as you go through life, it's just inevitable that you're going to face tough times. 2012 was a tough health year for me with two reoccurrences, one in my brain and another on my lung. Fortunately, my radiation oncologists were able to use two new noninvasive procedures to kill both tumors.

I am thrilled to tell you my pulmonary function tests are the best in nine years. My CT scans, PET scans, and MRIs are all stable. I have gained lots of "happy" weight, and most importantly, I feel great. I recently renewed my passport, and I hope to do it again on December 3, 2022.

Life is no longer about what I cannot do, but what I can do. I do not know if I am now living on borrowed time, but I do know when you have an illness like mine, you do not wait to do anything.

Last December, Michael, Rachel, and I took an amazing trip to Munich, Innsbruck, and Salzburg, and we came home with a lifetime of memories.

Life Goes On...Thankfully

I dedicate this anniversary to the two most precious loves of my life, Michael and Rachel. There are people in this world who light up the lives of those around them. Michael and Rachel are two of those people for me. I can't help but smile when they're around me, because they bring me so much joy. They continue to be my motivation and inspiration to do everything I can to beat this disease.

I know at times they must be afraid, but they continue to have the courage to live their lives to their fullest. Michael and Rachel have shaped my life and are the fiber of my being. My favorite three-letter Scrabble word will always be D-A-D.

Today, I want my friends and family to know how grateful I am to each of you. Thank you for your support, especially during some of the difficult times. Thank you for your phone calls and emails of encouragement. Thank you for your hugs, smiles, and prayers. I cannot imagine these past nine years without my friends and family on this journey with me.

Life goes on...thankfully.

Love,

Richard

Twenty-Six

Richard's Rays of Hope

I was not going to let the tenth anniversary of my illness pass without doing something extra special. I knew the numbers. In the ten years since I had been diagnosed, over a million and a half people had died of lung cancer. The fact that I was still alive sometimes felt like a miracle. I always believed I was alive because of a combination of chemistry, biology, timing, and good luck, and I repeated this mantra on my speaking tours.

Chemistry: Research teams all over the country were busy creating and testing astonishing new lung-cancer-fighting medicines.

Biology: I had a particular type of genetic material that benefited from the brilliant advances in personalized medicine to boost the immune systems to fight cancer.

Timing: I was diagnosed early, before the cancer had spread, which let me live long enough to benefit from these remarkable new treatments as they were developed.

Good Luck: No matter what, you need a little luck. Things go wrong despite the hard work and good intentions of teams of brilliant and well-meaning medical professionals. I had so much luck—fine medical professionals who cared about me, a strong constitution that enabled me to fight my disease, a supportive and loving network, and an enduring optimism that seemed to replenish itself just when I needed it most.

Life Goes On...Thankfully

Lung cancer is a terrible diagnosis. Not only is it often a silent killer, but the association with smoking damns the victim as somehow responsible—a traitor to his own cause. Being sick is bad enough; dealing with what feels like an accusation—"Are you a smoker?"—is an additional blow. So much of cancer is dark and foreboding and lonely. I wanted to make a statement about fighting an occult enemy with optimism, color, and inclusiveness.

My friend Jane, a movie producer and set designer, helped me develop my idea for a short, cheerful, and motivational video. She and I had been confidantes for a decade, ever since we had come out to one another, and in these last years, we had also shared the diagnosis of cancer. Jane had ovarian cancer, but even though she was sick and getting sicker, she was determined to help me.

My brother Ronnie came up with the idea of using chest X-rays as the canvas upon which to create our message. Another friend Zak, who had a national film-production company, agreed to be the filmmaker.

I narrated and starred in the video, which we called *Richard's Rays of Hope.* In it, we asked lung-cancer victims to get the actual films of their lung X-rays and "turn a negative into a positive." I got multiple copies of my chest X-rays and mailed them in great, big manila envelopes to people I loved along with a box of primary-color paints and some big paint brushes. I asked each person to create a picture with reds, yellows, blues, and oranges right on the X-rays, making simple designs of flowers, the sun, children—anything that made them happy. We filmed my loved ones receiving my chest X-rays and responding to my request to paint a picture right over my lungs.

My daughter, Rachel, painted a picture of me in a Superman costume, and on the chest, instead of the *S* for Superman, she painted a great big *D* for Dad. I just loved that one.

The activity itself was soothing, a reminder that there is healing in art, joy in creation, and a palette of color far from the darkness of disease. I featured my mother and father, brothers, and children expressing their true emotions about this battle we were all reluctant partners in fighting. There was an occasional, unstoppable tear, but also a lot of love and warmth.

We closed the film with a very short speech in which I encouraged people to try to stay alive until the next treatment comes along, because nothing is impossible. After all, I was proof positive.

Richard's Rays of Hope got tens of thousands of hits online, both on Facebook and on the lung cancer websites. It was one of the most important messages I could ever hope to share. Strangely, I did not care so much about the number of views, although I knew that was important. Instead, I treasured the hundreds of personal messages I received from people who saw the video and were motivated to go on with their fight.

One day, I was sitting in a diner in New York, when a pleasant-looking young man approached me. "Excuse me, but is your name Richard?"

"It is," I answered, intrigued by the young man.

"My name is Elliot," he said. "I recognize you from your video, *Richard's Rays of Hope*. My father has lung cancer. We watched that video online so many times. You have no idea how much we loved it and how much better it made us feel every time we saw it. My dad was so sick, and we kept watching the video when we were hanging around, when he was getting chemo, or when people came to visit. It gave us hope every time. I really want to thank you for it. How are you doing?"

I was happy to tell him that I was doing well. And of course, I wanted to hear about his father, who was, he said, "hanging in there."

The last time I checked, the video had gotten more than 55,000 views. I was never one for a legacy, but I was really proud that this video was part of mine.

Twenty-Seven

Chris

After David, there were a lot of guys. A few seemed promising, but I was still looking for Mr. Right. I began to wonder if I would just have to content myself with spending my time with my family and friends. I just could not handle another failed relationship. After all, let's face it, all those failures couldn't be blamed on the other guys alone, could they?

Then, one night I got a hit from OK Cupid. It was very sweet. The guy sounded really good, but he was from Stamford, Connecticut, and I had a strict rule about guys from Connecticut. Too far away for this New York City resident.

But upon reflection, I reminded myself that sometimes you need to break the rules. There was something about his friendliness and directness that appealed to me. He said he was looking for the right guy.

"The right guy?" I replied. "Maybe it's me? Who knows? Also, how tall are you? I do like a tall man."

"Is six foot three tall enough?"

We exchanged phone numbers. We spoke on the phone three nights in a row. The conversations were sweet, and there was a lot of laughter. I could tell he was smart, and his voice sounded sexy. We decided to meet. I didn't want to travel to Connecticut, stubbornly clinging to my prejudice. After all, I was a seasoned internet dater who weighed the likelihood of success against the time and effort expended to meet someone I actually liked.

"How about if we meet halfway?" I offered. "I know a diner that's perfect."

"Really? A diner? The lights are usually so harsh at night. I might have to wear a baseball cap. Why don't you let me make you dinner instead?"

Best little boy in the world caved. "Sure."

I met him at the train station in Stamford.

He was even more handsome than his profile picture. He was tall and slim with bright-blue eyes behind edgy eyeglasses. He had a sweet smile, even white teeth. He was wearing a white T-shirt, black running pants, and white socks with black flip-flops—a bit of a concern. But the clothes showed off a trim, muscular body, and he seemed so genuinely excited to see me, to know me, and to make me feel welcome that I just didn't care. When he took my hand, his hand was warm and strong. It felt sensuous and comfortable all at the same time.

This was fast. Despite the part of me that had grown skeptical over the years of three-dates-a-night-with-internet-maybes at Starbucks, I acquiesced to this attractive man, who kept looking at me with a big smile and great interest. I could feel the electricity in the air. A little voice in my head said, *Richard, he could be an ax murderer. Don't go to his apartment yet.* But a bigger, louder, pulsating Broadway show tune in my heart said, *This is it! Light the lights! Everything's coming up roses!*

I went to his place. He lived in a high-rise apartment not far from the train station. Nice building, doorman, real people around. So, he probably wasn't going to kill me. When we got off the elevator, walked down the hallway, and entered the apartment, I saw he had carefully planned the whole evening. The table was laid with colorful place mats, fresh flowers, and candles, and there was something waiting on the stove that smelled like hearth and home. He had gone out of his way to do all this for me.

Life Goes On...Thankfully

I was usually the one who took control of creating the atmosphere for romance, and it felt exciting and gratifying to be at the receiving end, especially from someone I immediately liked. He made no attempt to hide his excitement. I could see he was hoping our connection on the phone would turn into something that would not disappoint. He told me that he didn't date much, but he had had several long-term relationships. He was new but familiar, all at once. He bustled about the kitchen, stirring, tasting, fussing, all with the desire to please me. He kept up a steady banter, sweet and sexy. He put on some music, a John Pizzarelli jazz CD that I loved.

All of a sudden, I felt intoxicated. Could it finally be my time to fall in love with the right person? Was this the old romantic cliché—the moment I had waited for all my life?

I knew immediately and surely that I would marry him.

That was it. It felt easy, except it wasn't. It had taken an entire lifetime for me to get to Chris, a lifetime of avoidance and self-discovery, of love and disappointment, health and sickness, friends and, of course, family. But there he was, I had found him. I was ecstatic. When he touched me, I told him he felt so right, and I was not afraid to say the words.

He was not afraid to hear them, either. He said, "You are gorgeous, Richard," and I believed he was falling in love with me, too. We ate our dinner, but we didn't get to dessert until the middle of the night, when we came up for air and decided we were definitely both starving.

I called my mother that very day. I had to tell her.

"Mom, I've met someone. I swear I think I'm going to marry him. His clothing is a little twenty-something, and the dinner was not exactly perfect because he put the salad and the pasta on the same plate, but I just didn't care. He is sweet and warm and handsome and amazing."

"Really? Have I heard that before?"

Characteristically, she held back, reluctant to cheer me on in my blind haste for romance. But I knew no one in the world would be happier for me if he really was right.

Chris and I spent the next weekend together and almost every day that followed. It was a bit dazzling. First, there is no one in your life. Then, you move over, physically, mentally, happily, joyfully, making space in your day and your mind for someone you suddenly crave more than anything or anyone else in the world.

I had finally met someone more romantic than I was. Sometimes the love bewildered me.

Chris did not see cancer. Or illness or needles or bandages or a future in which these things might play a part. Chris saw only me.

I wasn't certain if I had the right to commit to a love affair with this man, for after all, would I not disappoint him? Loving me was not only risky, like all love affairs, but reckless. My illness had rendered me flawed, a man with an uncertain future, at best. But when I voiced my worries, he brushed my concerns aside. He had never been through an illness with me, but he said he didn't care, and I chose to believe him. "*You* will bury *me*," he said. Selfishly, I let him live with his self-deception. I loved him too much to do anything else.

Four months later, I signed a lease on an apartment in a Stamford high-rise so I could stop commuting up to Connecticut. After that, we were together every night.

Chris loved me with an intensity I had never experienced before. I understood that he was a person who thrived on intimacy. Chris had no noise in his life from family or friends. He could be very social, loved being around my large circle of friends and my family, but nothing made him happier than being alone with me.

A successful real estate agent, he worked very hard, perhaps harder than he needed to at his stage in the game. After a full day of work, his favorite evening occupation was to cuddle on the couch, watch TV, and do crossword puzzles together, one a night. He did not just want us on the same sofa; he wanted to share the same cushion and feel my body close to his. If he got up, it was to get Burt's Bees cream so he could massage my feet or my back or whatever part of my body caught his fancy. Yet, he was happy to go out with me and attend the theatrical productions I loved, thrilled to incorporate this lifelong passion of mine into his life.

We met each other's families almost immediately. Mine was already understandably wary because of the parade of men I had presented over the past ten years, but they were willing to go along with me, nevertheless. They wanted me to be happy, and they understood I could not be happy unless my lover was a part of my life. Rachel, now a mature woman in her early twenties, did ask me if I was moving along a bit too quickly, but I explained that cancer had made me reckless, because I did not want to waste one precious moment.

"What's the worst that will happen?" I asked. "I'll just take my things and move back to New York." We laughed. She had seen that show before.

Chris did not normally embrace so much family with his lovers. He'd had two previous partners for ten years each and had never met their families. I introduced mine the first week. I met his family the second week. His mother was very happy to meet me. She was a chain smoker with emphysema who was mostly housebound. Chris was afraid her cigarette smoke would hurt me, so the meeting was short, though pleasant.

Chris's maternal grandmother, Pola Weinbach Hoffman Stout, was Jewish, born in Poland in 1902. She left her family to go to Vienna in the 1920s, where she showed early promise as a clothing designer. A renegade, without the blessing of her family, she went to the United States, where she married the best-selling mystery writer Rex Stout and became a well-known, successful haute couturier and textile designer. Pola, celebrated for her beauty and talent, ultimately designed for First Lady Eleanor Roosevelt. She was the sole survivor of the family she left behind in Poland, who perished during the holocaust. The rest of Chris's family was Christian, but the distant stories of Poland and wartime loss had always intrigued him. He'd never followed up on them, though, until he met me.

He surprised me one day. "What if we decide to get married? If we do, I want to be married in a synagogue. No rabbi will marry us if I'm not Jewish, so I think I'm going to convert."

I was touched but a little hesitant. We were both grown men, both clear about our identities. In an age where gay marriage had become legal and widely accepted, changing his religion at the age of fifty-three seemed more than was necessary.

"You don't need to do that for me. I don't care if you're Jewish or not. I love you anyway. We can work it out without you converting."

But he knew my deep attachment to my religion, and he knew I would be happy to be married under a chuppah, the traditional canopy under which a Jewish couple is married. He did not listen to my demurrals and began a year-long series of weekly lessons with a rabbi on Judaism. He loved the course, and he loved the idea that we would be in a synagogue together. The lessons culminated in a ceremonial circumcision called a bris. For an adult male, instead of cutting the foreskin of the penis as is done for Jewish infants, the *moyle* (the Yiddish word for the person who performs the bris on Jewish males when they are eight days old) ceremonially draws blood by pricking the penis of an adult who has just emerged from a mikvah (a bath in a bathhouse typically visited by religious Jewish women once a month after they have completed a menstrual cycle).

When I heard about the bris, I laughed.

"Are you sure about this?" I asked. "You don't have to prick your prick for me. I love you regardless."

He would not be deterred. He was so taken with the lessons that he even chose our synagogue in Stamford, a more religious one than I would have selected myself. He loved going to services together. I went along with it all. No one had ever made such a sacrifice for me.

Life Goes On...Thankfully

Chris was a die-hard romantic. From the onset of our love affair, he sent me cards with love messages emblazoned all over them. He outdid even me when it came to cards. There were cards every night on my pillow, and if I went away, cards in my suitcase for me to open on each of the days we were apart.

His kind of love was humbling. I wanted to be able to accept his love completely, but sometimes I was so overwhelmed by it that I became frightened. I didn't know what to do with it.

One card read, "When you love what you have, you have everything you need." The inscription he wrote said, "This is what I have with you."

"Then can I have the TD bank account?" I asked, even though it hurt him. I needed to deflect the love, unsure what to do with it all.

I was the one used to giving. I thrived on it—the birthday cards, the phone calls, the crazy gifts, the faraway visits. Challenged as I was with lung cancer, I wanted to share my own experience with lung cancer patients to help them fight disease and despair. These things came easily to me. Now I had to learn to be a recipient, and to receive the love Chris offered in such abundance.

It came at me all the time. I, who had learned to appreciate every day in the hardest way, had found the greatest love of all, a man who loved me for myself, and I had to accept that and be open to it. In Chris, I had finally found what I had been searching for my whole life.

A Letter of Life

April 12, 2014
Dear Friends and Family,

Today is my tenth anniversary since being diagnosed with lung cancer. In some ways it seems like a lifetime ago when I heard my world-stopping words, "there is a spot on your lung." I dedicate today to the 1.5 million people who have lost their battles with lung cancer since I was diagnosed on April 12, 2004.

In honor of my tenth anniversary, I am producing a video titled *Richard's Rays of Hope*. I hope to turn a negative diagnosis into a positive way of life by raising awareness and hope for people impacted by cancer. I have asked my family to paint my actual chest X-rays and, as Walt Disney, who died of lung cancer, said, "Infuse a bleak reality with bright, happy colors." The finished versions will transform these discomforting images into wonderful rays of hope for cancer survivors and their caretakers. The video is in postproduction and will be released in a few weeks.

I am not always sure about why I chose to recognize these anniversaries. But I know I want to share that I am still in awe of my good fortune. As Bruce Feiler wrote in the *New York Times*, "I am among the lucky ones, at least for now. My biology has taken the chemistry. Like anyone in this situation, I have met many who never made it this far. I know everyone dies. But not everyone lives. I want to live." That's been my philosophy from the day of my diagnosis, and I hope to take with me whether my cancer comes back or not.

As I reflect on the past ten years, I ask myself to picture my life. Even with a diagnosis that is dire, I know it doesn't have to define my life. When I think about the last decade of my life, it was not

Life Goes On...Thankfully

wasted. It was a time filled with much happiness, enjoyable experiences, lots of laughs, and special people. At times, the cancer thing is very difficult, but my memories will be focused on ten really wonderful years.

Someone asked about giving me a gift today. But my gifts are truly my parents; brothers; sisters-in-law; brother-in-law; nieces and nephew; cousins; the gift of so many friendships; the gift of my children, Michael and Rachel; and now the gift of my partner, Christopher.

Christopher, the day I met you, my world changed remarkably. I love and like you profoundly and with absolute certainty. I discovered happiness beyond my wildest dreams with you. I am so lucky. Thank you for believing we will grow old together.

So, my teaching moment for today is we should all try to "be present." Be open to the moment that is unfolding before you, because ultimately, your life is made up of moments. So don't miss them by being lost in the past or anticipating the future. For me, those moments are the look on my mom's face when she sees me; Rachel's laugh when I do something silly; high-fiving Michael at a Jets football game; watching my nephew, Josh, put the last piece of puzzle into place; having a candlelight dinner on the bedroom floor and watching television with Chris. These are the things that shape my life. And I will never take them for granted.

I realize that some stories don't have a clear beginning, middle, and end. As I begin the next decade living with cancer, I continue to hope for the perfect ending. But I know I will continue to live my life with ambiguity. Life for me and all of us is about not knowing, having to change, taking the moment and making the best of it. And that is exactly what I am going to continue to do.

For the tenth straight year, I will end my letter by saying:
Life goes on...thankfully.
Here's hoping for many more!
Love,
Richard

Twenty-Eight

In Sickness and in Health

The *Richard's Rays of Hope* video occupied time and energy and provided so much joy and distraction that it was almost a surprise when I had another recurrence of cancer, and Chris had his first taste of what it was like to be with me when I was threatened by the disease. A PET scan revealed a new small spot near the pleura, which is the lining of the lung. Because I only had one lung, I was not a candidate for surgery. Instead, I was treated with stereotactic body radiation to kill the tumor. This type of radiation offers a very high dose, but a limited number of treatments aimed directly at the tumor instead of the more typical lower doses of radiation administered over a longer time period. I had something similar when I was treated for my earlier brain tumors.

Chris weathered it with stoicism and a healthy dose of denial.

While the treatment was successful, it also resulted in reduced pulmonary function for me. I began a regimen of daily exercise to regain my lost pulmonary function, and I began a new career as a gym rat. I was determined to beat back the compromises to my lung capacity, and I was so in love with Chris, I wanted to have a future like everyone else. I wanted to get married more than anything in the world.

I began to plot my marriage proposal to Chris. I called my friend Adam, the general manager of one of the area's best independent film theaters, the Avon Theater in Stamford. We were members and supporters of the theater, and he knew us well. Chris and I had seen movies at the Avon we both loved, such as *Elaine Stritch: Shoot Me, Boyhood, The Grand Budapest Hotel, Whiplash,* and countless others that made us happy we had left our spot on the couch.

"Can I rent the theater without breaking the bank?" I asked Adam. "I've got an idea for a marriage proposal."

"If you take it a couple of hours before the first showing of the day, I'll rent it to you for a song."

I secured the Wednesday before Thanksgiving in 2015 and told Chris that we were going to see a special 2:00 p.m. premiere of a film my son, Michael, now a producer, had been working on, called *The Imitation Game*. I told Chris we were getting cards to write our reviews on, and the cards would be there on our seats.

Then I called my buddy Zak, who had directed *Richard's Rays of Hope.*

He came to Stamford, went to the Avon Theater to set up hidden cameras and hidden microphones, and told me which seats to sit in so he could train the camera on us. Unbeknown to Chris, he was going to film us the entire time we were sitting in the theater.

I brought Chris to the theater on the appointed day at the appointed hour. He bought my story that we were seeing a special presentation of Michael's movie. In a classic case of almost ruining my surprise, he threw his coat on the wrong chair, covering one of the all-important mikes, but I restrained myself from removing it because I knew there was a backup mike somewhere, and I couldn't risk wrecking my surprise. We sat down and watched a rigged projector show trailers for the theater. After the last trailer, instead of *The Imitation Game*, a short film I had asked Zak to create came on. It was a collage of photos of Chris and me since we met, set to three different songs.

The last song was from *The Wedding Singer*, and was called, "Will You Marry Me?"

As Chris watched the last film, he began turning around, laughing, squirming, and crying. "What's going on? What is this?"

The final shot was a picture with the words, "Will you marry me?...Don't answer yet."

Then, as the lights were turned up just a bit brighter, I pulled out my proposal and read him the words I had prepared with painstaking love: "I, Richard Adam Heimler, promise to make my partner proposal to Christopher Maroc the last partner commitment I make for the remainder of my life here on earth. And I will not leave Chris Maroc for the duration of my life."

I also brought out champagne, flowers, and the ring I had stashed behind some seats, out of view.

Chris was laughing and crying, and so was I, and through his tears, Chris said, "Yes, yes, yes! I will marry you!"

I put the ring on Chris's finger, and we popped the cork right off the champagne. We had the whole thing on film ready to be shown at our wedding. We left the theater that day in a haze of tears and joy. I cannot remember feeling such love ever before.

The next day, we went to Chris's mother's house. She was a Jeopardy fanatic, and we broke the news with a personalized Jeopardy game. We had created a game with the question, "People Chris is going to marry."

"Who is Richard?"

She got it right, and so did we.

Life Goes On...Thankfully

A Letter of Life

April 12, 2015
Dear Friends and Family,

Today is my **eleventh anniversary** since being diagnosed with lung cancer. I dedicate today to the other 15 million cancer survivors in the United States. A person is regarded as a cancer survivor at the moment their disease is detected.

I am proud to be a survivor. One thing you accept as a cancer survivor is the realization you can never return to life as it was before the cancer diagnosis. Now, I am Richard with lung cancer. I can never go back to being just Richard again.

But being a cancer survivor doesn't have to define my life. I choose to live a little each day rather than die a little each day. In the book, Seabiscuit, Laura Hillenbrand wrote, "You do not throw a whole lifetime away because it is banged up a bit."

This was a difficult health year, as I was diagnosed with four new tumors. Fortunately, I started a new personal medicine, Zykadia, from Novartis. Three of the tumors responded well to the new medicine; two died, and one is shrinking. My radiation oncologist was able to kill the fourth tumor with pinpoint radiation. But the tumors and treatment reduced my pulmonary function. I am now exercising every day to increase my lung capacity and am thankful to have recovered 50 percent of the loss so far. And as Arthur Ashe said, "Start where you are. Use what you have. Do what you can."

When you have a diagnosis of cancer, you do think about your mortality, but I will not let cancer break my positive spirit. As I continue to live with cancer, I continue to live a full life. I saw a poem once that said "The tragedy of life does not lie in not reaching your goals. The tragedy of life lies in not having goals to reach for." I have lots of plans, and hopefully, nothing will interfere with them. I want to live my life like everyone else. What cancer has done for my life is to just make me pedal faster.

The sportscaster Stuart Scott, who recently passed away from cancer said, "You beat cancer by how you live, why you live and the manner in which you live. So live. Fight like hell and when you get too tired to fight, lay down and rest and let someone else fight for you." I am so fortunate to have my fiancé, Chris, in my life. Some days I do not feel good and when I see Chris come through the front door, my spirits are instantly lifted. He makes me feel safe and happy because I have someone wonderful to share good times, to survive the hard times, and to keep me company all the time. Most importantly, he accepts who I am and who I am not.

Finally, I am thrilled to announce our video, Richard's Rays of Hope, has exceeded all expectations. It has been viewed over 65,000 times around the world from the United States to Canada to Australia to Pakistan to Singapore. I believe we accomplished our goal of turning a negative diagnosis into a positive way of life by raising awareness and hope for people impacted by lung cancer.

In honor of my eleventh anniversary, please tell someone you love that you love them. For the eleventh straight year, I will end my letter by saying:

Life goes on…thankfully.
Here's hoping for many more!
Love,
Richard

PS: Please "share:"
My video, Richard's Rays of Hope, at http://youtu.be/Yb_yULgxaJ0
My Playbill.com story about my theater dates with Rachel, at http://www.playbill.com/news/article/defying-the-odds-living-with-cancer-and-loving-broadway-with-my-daughter-a-readers-story-343202

Twenty-Nine

An Ending

Shortly after our engagement, my father became very sick. He grew weak and dizzy, and after a series of tests, he was diagnosed with multiple myeloma, a form of cancer that makes it difficult to fight infection. My mother told me the news, speaking for him just as she had all my life. I was saddened, but it was for her more than for myself. I did not want her to lose the man she loved, to whom she had been married for more than sixty years. I did not want her to be alone.

For myself, I did feel the same old, tired, tattered wish that my father and I could have gotten along better. I had lived with that wish all my life, and its familiar reprise upon learning of his serious illness, gripped me with new sorrow. My relationship with my father was the one I always wished I could have changed. I tried so many times, but the odd tension between us never went away. I had finally come to believe that it never would—that the unreserved love I had with so many other men in my life, gay or straight, was never to occur with my father.

We all visited dutifully, helping him and my mother over the months of his illness, sharing her sorrow when she would express it. He passed away less than a year later. A crowd of people attended his funeral. I wept for my mother and for what I still wished might have been.

A Letter of Life

April 12, 2016
Dear Friends and Family,

Today is my twelfth anniversary since being diagnosed with lung cancer.

I knew this was going to be an eventful year, but I was hoping not medically. But cancer does not take its cues from me. The one pesky tumor on my lung decided to wake up. My dream team of doctors decided we needed to be proactive. In February, I entered a Pfizer clinical trial at Memorial Sloan Kettering. I am thrilled to report the first scan after six weeks of treatment showed the tumor shrinking by 14 percent!

Living with cancer for twelve years has conditioned me how to deal with adversity and keep a positive attitude. Even with this medical hiccup, my memories and dreams for this year will be focused on our recent European family vacation, Mike and Genae's engagement, and my upcoming wedding to Christopher. In my life, the sun will continue to come out tomorrow.

Sheryl Sandberg, chief operating officer of Facebook, after the passing of her husband wrote, "When tragedy occurs, it presents a choice. You can give in to the void or you can try to find meaning." When there is a void in life, she said, "and Option A is not available…let's kick the shit out of Option B." And that's what I will continue to do. At times, my life can be challenging, but I will always choose life and meaning.

This year, I dedicate my anniversary to my dad, who passed away in October. It is surreal to lose your first parent. But I know I was fortunate to have my dad in my life for fifty-five years. My dad's life goals were simple: marry his college sweetheart; create a life

Life Goes On...Thankfully

together; and since he was an only child, have a big family. I will always be grateful to my dad for his acceptance of my life decisions. He showed love, support, and joy, especially with Chris in my life. The philosopher William James said, "The best use of a life is to spend it for something that will outlast it." My dad spent his life for his family, and I know because of him, we will flourish as a family for generations to come.

Finally, when you live with cancer, you think about life-cycle moments and hope to be a part of those amazing milestones. I love life and don't want to spend any of it saddened by the loss of what I might miss. As Julianne Moore's character in the movie *Still Alice* said, "Live in the moment; that's really all I can do." My wish to anyone reading this letter is to have the greatest appreciation of life. Do not take any day for granted. Celebrate your birthdays, anniversaries, and every cloudy day. We are all lucky to have them.

For the twelfth straight year, I will end my letter by saying:

Life goes on...thankfully.

Here's hoping for many more!

Love,

Richard

Thirty

The Wedding

I woke each morning wondering if I was dreaming. I could not imagine a happiness any greater. Despite the many times I thought I'd found love in the past, I knew that Chris and I each found what we longed for. I was fifty-six years old. I didn't know what lay ahead. But I knew I wanted to be with Chris for all of it. We were giddy with love.

I knew it was selfish of me and possibly cruel, but Chris loved me in a way I couldn't turn away from. I put my fears and hesitations aside and lived in the present as much as I could. Each day, like each night, I was surprised by his intensity. The cards continued to come—on my bed and under my pillow, in my clothing drawers, in the glove compartment of my car, in my morning email, and later in the afternoon, in my US mailbox. I basked in it, felt like I was swimming in it, and for me, best of all, our sexual energy matched our romantic energy. His touch was still as electric to me three years after we met as was mine to him.

I felt like Pippin, the character in my favorite Broadway show when I was a child. Pippin longed to find his rightful place in the world. I felt that I had finally found that place beside Chris. I thought often of the lyric, "I want my life to be something more than long" from *My Corner of the Sky*. I knew my cancer advocacy helped others, but I felt untold joy in finding a love that was right for me after all my struggles. My dream had finally come true.

Life Goes On...Thankfully

I kept reminding myself to make every day count, to live each day to the fullest. Sometimes my mindfulness got waylaid when I saw some of the houses Chris was selling. He was constantly bombarded with listings of homes that beckoned with the promise of future happiness. Sometimes I saw the perfect house for us, and I dreamed that we could buy it and live happily ever after within its warm embrace. But I stopped myself and reminded myself that we were ecstatic right where we were, and we would take our love one step at a time, without the complications of a glorious new love nest that Chris might have to live in alone someday.

Sometimes I woke in the night, routed from sleep by a shooting pain or an anxious thought, only to find Chris breathing evenly right beside me, with an arm around me or a leg thrown over one of mine. Mostly he was asleep, but sometimes I woke to find him looking straight at me, as much in love with me as I was with him. When our eyes met, we giggled like children, unable to believe our great fortune; or we stroked each other, gathering heat, and made love. In these moments, I pictured my heart expanding in my poor battered chest, or I imagined that inside me was the ghost of my old lung and that it was filled with joy, which I breathed in and out, in and out, an expanding and contracting magnum of happiness from which I drew sustenance as precious as oxygen.

Chris had never been married, so I wanted him to have the wedding he'd always dreamed of. Where I might have gone for a great big bash, he imagined a small, intimate ceremony in a beautiful, rustic retreat. And so that's what we did.

We married in the spring, three years after we met, in an outdoor wedding in the verdant hills of Connecticut, in a field of flowers, beside a crystalline lake, in front of an historic red barn. We were officially united by the rabbi from our synagogue under a cloth canopy—the traditional Jewish chuppah, which symbolizes the home that the Jewish couple will build together. The chuppah was held aloft by my three brothers and my son.

We walked down the aisle, accompanied by the voice of our cantor. She sang a song that we both loved, one of the most popular wedding songs in the world, "What a Wonderful World," in a clear and penetrating soprano.

During pauses in the music, everyone could hear sniffling and the sound of repressed sobs. Everyone there knew the journey we both had taken to reach that moment. They knew my battles with illness and failed love affairs; they knew our commitment to Judaism and Tikkun Olam, to making our world a better place; and because they were such close friends and family, they also knew our failures; and they loved us for our happiness and bravery.

Of course, we wrote our own vows.

Chris broke down as he spoke, barely able to choke out the words he had so painstaking prepared.

"We will celebrate each day as husband and husband. I promise to take care of you and love you completely. I will make my home in your heart from this day forward. We do not dictate what will occur. But I believe in miracles, and that kings and queens, castles, and dragons do exist."

My own carefully chosen words were, "Chris, when I met you that was fate. Falling in love with you was out of my control. You have surpassed my dreams. You think about me all day; you run across the hall with a big smile and a hug me like you haven't seen me for days, even though it might only be a few hours. I cannot guarantee you the future; things might not go as planned; but I will love you every day of my life. I am truly lucky in love today."

In the tradition of Jews from time immemorial, the male stomps on a glass and breaks it after the ceremony. It's a symbol of the destruction of the Jewish temples in early history, but it also has come to symbolize the fragility of relationships and the need to cherish them. It is a joyful moment, the moment when the marriage ceremony ends, and the couple is ready to face the audience and the world. Like all traditions, though, it needed to grow with the times. So we both had glasses, and we stomped on them together to the delight of the audience, which immediately broke out in song and cheers of mazel tov.

After the ceremony, I circulated. My best and oldest friend, Sam, was there. He had doctored me through countless emergencies.

"You finally did it," he said, with tears in his eyes. "You've made even me cry."

My friend Marcy had come east from California. "Make every moment count, Richard. We always want to be in control, but we're not; so let's just embrace happiness where we can!"

My dear ex-wife, Jodi, to whom I would always feel I owed so much of my life—and who had found her own new man—said with real warmth, "It's so hard to believe we've made it this far, Richard. We are not to be taken lightly. We are truly a force."

Rachel, my heart and my soul, smiled at me, letting me know yet again that I was and would always be her hero. "Good job on the vows, Dad. I could not stop crying. But they are tears of joy, thank goodness. I'm truly happy for you and Chris!"

Michael hugged me and said, "Dad, no matter what, I'm not calling Chris 'Dad.' I've got enough with just one."

Thirty-One

Where There Is Breath, There Is Life

The days that followed were dreamlike to me. I couldn't wait to be with Chris, and he felt similarly. We kept our independent lives, each busy with our work and commitments, but we found renewed joy each time we came home, gluttonous with love. In Chris, I had finally found what I'd sought all my life. I felt justified that the path I had taken had led me to this place. I basked in it, gloried in it, and felt again and again that our love was *beshert*, a Hebrew word that means *destined*. We socialized, attended musicals and dramatic shows, visited friends, and shared each other's families, but home was where we found our deepest happiness.

We had to make room in our lives for my medical treatments, however; the occasional emergencies and the slow, aching realization that I was not feeling as strong as I once did. I fought the feeling, often reluctant to say even one word about it, but I knew that Chris let me have my peace because he loved me so and wanted to give me whatever he could, and because he did not want to believe that our love was threatened.

When my right lung was removed, I was left with sharply reduced breathing capacity. I worked diligently in pulmonary therapy for months after my surgery, and I soon was able to breathe almost as efficiently as anyone with two lungs did. For

Life Goes On...Thankfully

many years after the surgery, I was able to ski, travel, and go to spin classes. The pulmonary therapy worked.

People with normal lungs have an oxygen capacity of 48 percent in the left lung, which has two lobes and 52 percent in the right lung, which has three lobes. But after thirteen years with one lung and many recurrences of cancer, my most recent tests showed a 26 percent breathing capacity.

I refused to accept the decline. I wanted to get back to over 35 percent. I labored for several hours at home every day, performing time-consuming breathing exercises morning, noon, and night—in and out, in and out—blowing into a mouthpiece attached to a small plastic column in which a ball moved up and down according to the strength of my inhalations and exhalations. With each breath, I tried to break new ground, the upper reach of the ball in the column a virtual time line for my longevity. The higher the ball, the longer my life.

The pulmonary center I went to for follow-up was one floor above my health club. Naturally slim, I always hated going to any gym, where I felt like a lightweight compared with the men around me. When I did go, I always counted down the boring moments till I could leave. But all that had changed. I embraced my workout. I became a gym rat with cancer. I used the treadmill, bicycle, and rowing machine and worked out on the weight machines. I loved my routine and the sense that I was doing what I could to help myself.

I had pulmonary therapy three times a week at the pulmonary rehabilitation center. Most of the people there were twenty years older than me, suffering with chronic lung diseases like bronchitis or emphysema. Despite the huffing and puffing we all engaged in, I never got discouraged. I reminded myself that I was prolonging my life with every breath.

I left the gym one morning and headed for the elevator to go upstairs. An attractive, sweeping spiral staircase also provided access to the second floor, but I didn't have the lung capacity to climb it. I saw a woman carrying weights in her hands climbing up and down the staircase for her exercise. She didn't have to think twice about her ability to climb up. I had no choice but to think about mine.

Part of my incentive to work out so much was for those who loved me. I wanted to be in the best shape I could for them. I knew plenty of people who said *enough is enough* when they were sick. But I would not give up. I knew I was fighting a battle with one lung tied behind my back, because even as I strengthened my breathing capacity, I had to take aggressive, caustic medications to keep the cancerous tumors that spotted that lung in check.

The growing need for oxygen was changing my ability to move about freely.

I had to think carefully about where I went and how I would get there. Could I drive? Where would I park? Should I take the train? An Uber? How far did I have to walk to reach my destination? One block? Two blocks? An unthinkable three?

I tried desperately to keep my anxiety under wraps from everyone I loved.

~

One Wednesday, I met Rachel in New York for a matinee. The subway stop at Grand Central Station was three stories underground and had no elevator. I couldn't climb the stairs anymore, so I drove instead, right into the hellish traffic. But even that was complicated. If the parking garage I selected was full, I might have to use one with a sloped, subterranean parking level, and I would be unable to climb up and out to the street. I knew all the restaurants near the theaters. I made a reservation close to the theater so I wouldn't have to walk too far.

Elaborate planning, all to make my life appear normal.

"Dad," said Rachel, "I just read a review of a new restaurant that's supposed to be great, and is right near the theater, just a block or two away."

"Sure, love to go!" I said, my heart sinking.

I never refused her. I just walked a bit more slowly and left a few moments earlier to forestall the moment when I would have to tell her I hadn't the strength to walk. I feared it would break her heart.

Despite all the daily exercises, my lung capacity decreased from 26 percent to 22 percent over the next six months. I was sleeping poorly because I lacked the proper oxygen level. I had no choice but to get a home oxygen machine to use at night, and with it, I began to sleep much more comfortably.

I loved going to bed, just to get hooked up. It was as if I were a junkie. Even as I inhaled hungrily for the respite the additional oxygen provided, I fretted that supplemental oxygen put me on the list of the fully disabled. I was going the wrong way.

A newlywed, I feared turning my home into a hospital. There are few turnoffs greater than a sick room. Oxygen machines are noisy. All that pumping is annoying. I did not want Chris to think about it all the time, especially in the bedroom.

I put the clunky oxygen machine in the spare bedroom next to the master and called the cable guy—well, the O_2 equivalent of the cable guy. I got extra lengths of clear plastic tubing, the equivalent of an extension cord for oxygen delivery, and had the handyman in my building snake the tubing along the baseboards like old-fashioned cable lines. The oxygen line wended its way along the walls, slithered through a closet in the spare room, and then emerged from the back of the closet into the adjoining master bedroom, where it was tacked to the baseboard on my side of the bed.

Chris only had to see me wearing a very small, clear-plastic piece in my nose. I told myself he almost did not know it was there.

Thirty-Two

Making Memories

When I was a little kid, I spent a lot of time thinking about what to get my mother for her birthday. I loved her so dearly that I wanted her present to be really special. I agonized between surprising her with something she might not like or just asking her for a few ideas.

One Saturday morning, before my grandparents came over, I asked her what she wanted for her birthday. I hoped she would tell me so I could ask my grandmother for help going to a store for a present.

She laughed, and said, "Sweetheart, I don't need anything at all. Why don't you make me a special picture?"

And that's what I did. I got out my paints and my brushes and some glue and some glitter, and I made her the kind of picture every kid who grew up in safety and security makes…a house with a few windows and a door, a tall green tree, a blue sky with clouds and a sun, and stick figure of a woman holding hands with a little stick figure of a boy. I emblazoned hearts on the picture and presented it to her with great fanfare. She told me she would cherish it forever, and I believed her. I know she kept it stashed in a keepsake box for years after I gave it to her. I understood from her that real love came straight from the heart, and a personal message said the most.

Life Goes On...Thankfully

When it came time for my first wedding anniversary with Chris, I felt the same urge to do something special for him. I decided to make a scrapbook of our first year together, highlighting something joyful from each month of our one-year marriage. I knew he'd love it, because each of those moments really did come straight from my heart. I was finally able to give and receive love the way I'd wanted to my whole life. Our existence was precious and precarious. I felt vulnerable in a way I never had before, and I desired to live each beautiful day to its fullest with my adoring husband. The love was there, a constant in both of our lives, like a beating heart.

My first stop was Michael's, a huge craft superstore with everything you could dream of for art projects. I looked through the scrapbooks that celebrated every significant event in life and rejected the wedding choices with covers that boasted, "I'll love you forever," because I just couldn't promise that.

Instead, I selected a big fat scrapbook that echoed one of my lifelong mantras with the word "Memories" scrawled across the cover. Then I went up and down the aisles like a shopper in the TV show *Supermarket Sweeps*.

I bought two three-inch pearl-studded stickers, one a *C* and one an *R* and a big red heart for the first page. Then I bought a bunch of embellishments such as "I love you" stickers, wedding-themed stickers, football-game stickers, travel stickers, and even medical-themed stickers like stethoscopes, hypodermic needles, a medical bag, and all the usual kitsch. I bought stickers for each month of the year and laughed with glee when I found "First Halloween" and "First Valentine's Day" because I had a treasure trove of photos for those.

I bought sparkle glue and glitter pens and chuckled the whole time I walked up and down the aisles, knowing Chris would have a meltdown when I gave him this gift.

Once back at home, I searched through my digital photos from each month since we were married and had a selection printed at the local drug store. I found the memorabilia box from our wedding, a veritable treasure trove for a scrapbook, and selected the invitation, a napkin with our names and the words *Lucky in Love* on it, a menu, RSVP cards, a few pressed flowers, and the two grooms that stood atop our wedding cake. I found a picture of Barbra Streisand that I paired with a photo taken of us at one of her concerts in Philadelphia, and some tickets from our last trip to San Francisco. I added some food labels to denote our latest obsession, eating organic, and I put my wish for our second year on the last page.

"I wish for more nights in hotel rooms and fewer nights in the E.R.
Love, Richard."

When I gave the scrapbook to Chris, I made him guess what it was.

"Attaché case?"

I scoffed. "That's too businesslike."

When he finally guessed and opened it, he did not disappoint me. He was in tears by page three.

His gift to me was a NutriBullet, the kind of atomic blender that turns acres of fresh fruits and vegetables into one super drink. To me it was yet another pledge to do whatever it took to make me healthy, so we could continue our love and lives together. I loved it.

It was a wonderful anniversary. I felt lucky. Lucky in love, lucky I found him. Lucky he married me. He loved me in the way I always dreamed of, and I was finally able to accept that love.

What can you say about a guy who will give you a shot in the behind that's already black and blue from previous injections and just say—and mean it—"You've got the cutest tush in the world"?

Thirty-Three

Turning Point

I was stuck in a fast-moving current, gasping for air, looking for a tree root or overhanging branch to grab. But each time I thought I might have found a lifeline, my grip was torn away by the force of the water.

I puttered around my apartment, slowly preparing for the day, feeling rueful about the length of time it took me to get ready.

I used to jump out of bed, take a few minutes to get dressed, run a brush through my hair, take a quick look in the mirror, and off I would go. Now every movement was labored, deliberate, cautious. I had to move slowly, or I would get dizzy and short of breath, or most frightening, feel my heart pumping in my chest. I had to get my medications—swallow some, inject some—then take a shower, all in agonizingly slow motion.

I often made jokes about how good I looked to others. Like my Facebook page, my presentation was all a camouflage—no one really could imagine I was so sick. Now each morning I faced the truth in the grueling process of a slow awakening, a sunrise battle with the night's medication hangover, and the steady routine of shots and meds required to get me going. I was grateful Chris was an early riser and loved to be out of the house at 5:30 a.m. so he could hit the gym and then get to his office. He didn't have to see me rouse myself or watch my torturous morning routine.

Despite my growing concerns about the breathing constraints that were literally suffocating me, I refused to curtail my activities. I insisted Chris and I attend the singer Betty Buckley's concert about an hour's drive away. I had seen her perform many times on Broadway, and she was a favorite of mine. When she sang, I was transfixed, my heart swelling with emotion along with her magnificent soprano. When she sang one of her standards, "Children Will Listen," about the way children are forever shaped by the things their parents do and say, I felt grateful for every agonized moment I spent upending all our lives but then repairing the rupture. I knew our family had endured. Renewed and fortified by the performance, I resolved to continue my struggle, no matter the odds. I would not give up. Chris and I drove home from the show ecstatic.

The next morning, I awoke to a choking sensation. I could not get enough air. The oxygen from the tank was flowing as it should but was no longer enough. Panic rose in a swell so frightening it felt to me as if I would rather just die. Chris had gone off to the gym as usual. I knew I had no choice. I had to go to the Emergency Room at Stamford Hospital.

I refused to call 911, even though a less stubborn person would not have hesitated. Instead, I moved slowly and with deliberation. I instructed myself to breathe as deeply as I could to oxygenate my body. I dressed slowly and put on a comfortable pair of loafers. I skipped the socks, the morning meds, and the shower, and slowly headed for my car, all the while telling myself I had survived much worse. I felt grateful to live in a modern high-rise apartment that not only had beautiful views of Long Island Sound but also offered quick and easy access to the hallway elevator and the garage, where my car was parked in a space for handicapped drivers. The only time I thought my plan was impossibly harebrained was when I had to shift the bulky oxygen tank from its wheeled carrier into the car. I could barely lift it.

Perhaps I was thinking of my kids or Chris. Perhaps I was thinking of my mother and my fear of what she would suffer with the loss of her son. Somehow, I got the strength I needed. I got myself into the car and drove down the spiral exit ramp and onto the street. The hospital was just a few miles from my house. I prayed I would not cause an accident.

I pulled into the ER entrance and, with my last ounce of strength, asked the attendant, "Would you please get me a wheelchair?"

I was immediately shepherded through the waiting room and given a private cubicle in the ER. The rush of staff, agonizingly familiar to me, swooped in, treated and stabilized me. The diagnosis: mucus on my lung and my esophagus. Treatment: an antibiotic. It seemed so simple, but it was a whole day's discovery project.

And as of yet, none of my family knew where I was. Chris kept sending me texts. "Where is my husband? WHERE IS MY HUSBAND?"

I knew he was at work. I didn't want to worry or frighten him, so I dodged him.

I finally got home to find him pacing the living room. He was near distraction, angry and tearful at once.

"Richard, you simply cannot do this," he said. "You have to call me and tell me what's happening. You *have* to! I'll listen to you if you tell me not to come to the ER, but I need to know in real time when this happens. I've been sick with worry."

"The tests take forever. It's not worth coming. You know I'll tell you if there's anything important."

I was desperately trying to sound as if my behavior was reasonable, but I knew it wasn't. This was not the first time I had gone off radar, reluctant to give him bad news. He was asking me to stop protecting him, and I wasn't sure I could ever stop shielding him from pain, especially when I was the source of that pain. I didn't want to argue with him, and I didn't want to listen to him, even though I knew he was right. I just wanted to lie on the sofa and have him cuddle up next to me, hold me, and forgive me.

Ultimately, that's exactly what he did. He loved me too much to hold a grudge.

~

I felt better a few days later. My mother came up to visit from her new home in Florida. Happily, I didn't need to be on oxygen that day. My mother could see immediately that I was weaker. She acutely eyed my deliberate and slowed motions, but she didn't have to see me with the oxygen tank in tow.

She was full of news about my brothers and their families, and we spent some time confirming details of a trip we were planning for the upcoming summer, which we both were looking forward to. We were planning to go to Berlin with Rachel and Michael and his wife. I was determined to go, despite my recent setback, but as always, I bought trip insurance as a backup.

As soon as she left, trouble began anew. I had a routine appointment at Memorial Sloan Kettering for an MRI and a brain scan, part of my usual schedule of follow-ups. I had no choice but to bring my oxygen tank with me. I could no longer get along without it.

During my exam, the staff and I sifted through the list of possible reasons for my increased difficulty breathing. The Stamford ER doctor had seen mucus, but the Sloan Kettering doctor did not. Maybe the antibiotic administered the week before was kicking in.

I was also offered the idea that allergies might be behind the breathing problems. Many people succumb to allergies in the spring, I was told. Some are so afflicted that they take to their beds, popping antihistamines and avoiding the outdoors at all cost. Could I be one of them? Wouldn't it be lovely to think so?

The simple human drama of allergies would be such a relief.

A year earlier, just days before Michael's wedding, I'd had a sudden bout of diverticulitis that put me in the hospital. It was ironic, but at the time, despite my extreme physical discomfort, I was relieved to have just a regular old nonlife-threatening kind of illness that could be treated and resolved. A guy who's beaten cancer for thirteen years has earned the right to scoff at allergies and diverticulitis.

And like the Superman Rachel had drawn on my *Richard's Rays of Hope* video, I did bounce back and make it to the wedding.

But I couldn't dispel the lurking fear that something dreadful was happening. I measured the state of my health by the amount of oxygen assistance I needed and by the length of the cord that connected me to my life support. At home, I had to use a twenty-five-foot plastic tube connected to my tank so I could move around the apartment freely. I was tethered, squirming under the yoke of this new reality, hoping it was a short-lived setback. But whenever I cut myself loose from the tether, I struggled. I could not describe the relief I felt when I attached myself to my tank and the discomfort subsided.

I didn't want anyone I loved to know about my dependence on the oxygen. Before, only Chris had known that I was more comfortable at night with an oxygen assist—only two small tubes he could barely see. The portable oxygen I now needed during the day was a screaming sign that I was deteriorating. It was the decline I'd feared all along. I still wanted to control it, to force-fit this setback into my timeline. A line from the play, *The Great Comet*, often came to my mind: "I don't want to die while I'm still living."

To distract myself, I worked from home, busy on the phone with a list of synagogue members to contact for a fund-raising drive. The phone conversations calmed me down.

"Hello, John, it's Richard. You may remember you made the unfortunate comment to me in shul last week that you enjoy spending your time in the synagogue and are so glad you joined..."

I was competent and surefooted in my role as a fund raiser. I understood firsthand the joy of belonging to a welcoming community and the disturbing and dislocating feeling of being an outcast. "We are having an excellent speaker on a topic I know you are interested in..."

    I laughed and cajoled members to remember their responsibilities to the synagogue and to the Jewish causes they supported. It wasn't difficult. I knew most people want to be a part of a place they respected and that respected them, whether they were flush with money or not, straight or gay. This was a responsibility I loved, and as long as I could get the breath, I wanted to perform it. It was easy to speak at home where no one could see the long, clear-plastic tube that connected me to the large oxygen tank in my bedroom.

    In between the calls to synagogue members, I continued my practice of connecting with my friends and family by sending birthday, anniversary, get well, and unexpectedly amusing risqué cards just to let people know they were important to me. I always loved to surprise my friends. I'd once told my friend Gary to meet me at Penn Station on his birthday and dumfounded him with a private ride on a double-decker bus to the famed Apollo Theater in Harlem, because he told me he loved the show *Dreamgirls*. That was a flashy surprise, but I pulled all kinds of lesser stunts that were equally appreciated. The calls and the cards calmed me, and I could let go of some of my dread.

    Then, good news. I got a late-afternoon call from one of the staff members at Memorial Sloan Kettering. My recent tests at the hospital showed there was no fluid in my lung, which meant my heart was working and my lung was functioning. My spirits lifted. Perhaps the cat with nine lives was back. I had won many unlikely victories, and I resolved to keep strong and retain my equanimity. So far, I was not giving in to illness, and now I had the medical facts to bolster my stubborn insistence on living my life. When Chris came home, I surprised him with a bouquet of shaggy pink peonies, his favorite flower, and a basket of Burt's Bees products so we could give each other massages.

Life Goes On...Thankfully

The next day, I went to the gym and worked out. I had to wear my oxygen, but I was able to do forty-five minutes on the treadmill. Victory.

Until I got home. I couldn't breathe and felt chest pain.

My first call was to Brian, one of my oldest friends. I spoke to Brian almost every day of my life. Brian was a cardiologist, and many times dissected with me the complications of my illness. He provided not only sound advice but inordinate comfort. "Go to a cardiologist right now, Richard," he said. "Don't wait."

Instead, I hung up and began to clean.

Somehow, the delay helped me dampen my spiking anxiety. I cleared my desk. I put away all the clean dishes in the dishwasher. I freshened the towels in the bathrooms after I did the laundry. I had bought some saucepans from Home Goods for Chris, but he was very particular about his pans, so I put the one he wanted to return in a bag and added to it a quilt my mother had sent me that I wanted to return to her. UPS was right around the corner from Home Goods, so I had it all ready.

Years ago, when Jodi and I were traveling, we asked some friends to keep an eye on our house while we were gone. We left the house immaculate, and when they came to check on the house, they were incredulous that we were so neat. They messed up our bed and squirted ketchup on some dishes and put them in the sink. Then they took pictures just to make us laugh.

Maybe it's a Jewish thing to clean up before you go. In *Fiddler on the Roof*, Goldie swept the floor just before leaving her home because of a forced evacuation of the Jews from their small Russian village. Her husband, Tevye, asked, "What are you doing, Goldie? Sweeping for the Cossacks?" She didn't care. She wanted it neat. She had her self-respect, despite the eviction. She was closing an important chapter in her life.

When the house was clean, I was ready. I called the cardiologist's office, said I was having chest pain, and went in. I did not call Chris. I knew he'd begged me to, but I just couldn't do it. The appointment took a long time, but I was cleared of a cardiac assault and then told to go to the Emergency Room at Stamford Hospital just to make sure other vital parts of my body were not betraying me. I did as I was told.

At the ER, they remembered me from the week before and suggested inpatient admission.

I considered it but rejected their cautious approach. I didn't have time for another inpatient stint. I still had to go to Home Goods and UPS, and I had my work at the synagogue and a lunch date the next day, not to mention tickets for *Hello, Dolly* starring Bette Midler on Broadway in just two days.

Half joking, I said, "How about if you just rule out a few things—pulmonary emergencies, blood clots, and infections?"

They checked what felt like a hundred things in that routine ER visit, and I hoped, while I was waiting, that I wouldn't die in the everlasting process. In between the flurry of tests and evaluations, I spent my time in the ER making phone calls, none of them to Chris, whom I still refused to worry with yet another ER visit.

My first call was to the doctor's office at Sloan Kettering, where I had been just the day before. I wanted to let them know I had been experiencing chest pain and get their feedback on any new test results or impressions of what could be wrong. I'd known them all long enough to expect a useful medical impression. One of the medical assistants I knew took my call.

She said, "Well, Richard, the tumor *is* growing, so it's probably the cancer making it harder for you to breathe."

I couldn't believe what I had just been told. That was the first time I had heard the tumor in my lung was growing. The good news I'd received just a day before from the very same office was premature because it was incomplete—the results of one of the other tests had just come in. Information was not supposed to be delivered that way, of course, but there it was. The tumor was growing. Which meant my medication was failing, and I was at a crossroad I could no longer deny.

My first thought was that I would have to tell my mother, Chris, and my kids. The second thought was one I had not had in a long time. *My luck has finally run out. I'm dying.*

I had so much unfinished business. I didn't want to focus on this news. I could not absorb it yet.

Still in the ER, I called my old college friend Rita, who had been texting me repeatedly from her doctor's office. She had just been diagnosed with Stage IV lung cancer—an unlucky coincidence—and was seeking my opinion on the treatment options she was exploring. I was expert to her novice, pro to her Little League. I knew she was hoping that my story would be her story, that she would get at least the thirteen years I had gotten. I didn't want her to know I was in the ER. I purposely moved to an area where she would be unable to hear the sounds of the hospital, the beeping, the overhead speakers, the background of voices.

We talked about her latest visit with her doctor. She was having trouble understanding the choices. I understood all her issues well. It's hard to learn something new and important when you feel you are doing all you can to walk tall through the gauntlet, and the words are just blows raining down on you. It's all you can do to put one foot in front of the other when you're frightened and angry and resentful.

I tried to clear up her medical questions and her drug options, translating the language of cancer that the novice must learn to understand quickly. She was evaluating her options, but it was clear she needed to be on chemotherapy. The sooner, the better.

"I know you're scared," I said. "You have to try to see past your fear. The hardest is the hair. You can get a great wig—that part can be less awful than you realize. Maybe you want to become a blonde for the first time in your life."

"I don't want a wig! I hate the very thought of it! I don't believe this! I want my life back!" She began to cry. "I want my job that I hate, my chardonnay at night, my fights with my impossible son—my comfortable, boring, imperfect life!"

"Rita, I know, believe me. But your most important job right now is to stay alive," I said from a hallway in the ER. "I know it's no fun to feel the world reeling round and round, but it does stop."

I sympathized with her panic over her son's future, the terror and shame of having lung cancer, the humiliation of baldness, and seeing the discomfort of almost everyone you run into. But for the first time, I could feel that I was distancing myself from her. Her pain penetrated my own sense of fragility. Where once I was strong for both of us, I now needed to dig deeper than ever to be the person she needed me to be. I thought I could help her, but I found it frightening to talk to someone so fearful of dying when I believed I was dying myself.

Next, I called my friend Jane, who was battling cancer as well. We had a lunch date the next day. I was considering canceling because I didn't want her to see me with oxygen. She thought I was a pillar of strength, because for so long, I did not have to use oxygen and she had to. She had always admired my ability to travel and move around. She rarely left her house, so great was her fear of going out at all. I got lucky; she canceled instead.

Finally, all my tests were done. They sent me home from the ER. This time, knowing the tumor was growing, I had to tell Chris. It broke my heart. We had been married for just one year.

When I got home, he was preparing dinner. It was lean, grass-fed chicken and a variety of green vegetables that were superfoods. Perhaps it was kale sprinkled with sesame seeds, accompanied by a side of farro, or some other such hyperhealthy fad. A friend in California swore organic nutrition was the cure-all for her own ailments. I was always a spaghetti-and-meatballs kind of guy, so the sudden embrace of these kinds of foods was a lifestyle change. But Chris loved the idea of making me shakes and feeding me nutritious meals.

Over dinner, I drew a breath. "Chris, I have daunting news. The latest test showed that the tumor on my lung is growing, and for sure my medication is no longer working. I'm going to have to start a new treatment."

Chris put his fork down. He blinked back the tears that suddenly sprang to his eyes. "We'll never give up, you know. We will find the next treatment together. You've beaten every setback so far, and you will this time, too. We will find the right doctor and the right drug for you, no matter where we have to search. I'm not going to lose you now."

I didn't tell him how frightened I was. I didn't tell him what I already knew—that I was the one who had to take my own advice now. I would have to try to stay alive until the next miracle drug that was right for me came down the pipeline. But I knew that this time, I didn't have the luxury of waiting too long. The pipeline had to be short.

Thirty-Four

Superman to Clark Kent

I've had a lot of experience living two different lives. First as a gay man who had to face his truth and come out to everyone he knew and loved, and then as a sick man who wanted to protect others from the dangers of loving a person with a deadly illness.

I loved being Superman and doing the impossible. I loved being the person who made others laugh and feel loved and valued, the unlikely hero who conquered illness and lived a rich and full life despite all the odds.

When I came out, I was lucky. Jodi never turned her back on me. She made my new life possible. And, oddly, this ferocious killer cancer also helped me.

I knew many people were shocked and uncomfortable with the pain I caused my children and my wife by disrupting the status quo in our tightly knit, family-oriented community. In part, they forgave me because they liked me or wanted to see themselves as liberal. But all my hard work trying to mitigate the communal surprise and dismay of my coming out amounted to very little compared with the rocket booster of sympathy I got when I was diagnosed with lung cancer. People were uncomfortable with my choices, but they didn't think I deserved a death sentence.

What did I believe I deserved?

Would it be better that I lived to ninety but was less happy? I'd made it to almost sixty, and look at my riches. I was a man committed to living a Jewish life, but I didn't really believe in an almighty God who had ultimate power—or in heaven, either, for that matter. But I did believe in the power of love and the joy and tragedy of opening oneself up to love. Each time I suffered anxiety and fear, I resolved that even though I couldn't really know the future, I did not need to. I just needed to live as many moments, hours, days, weeks, months, and years as I could.

I began to calculate my next options for treatment, slim as they were. I knew I had exhausted all the latest medicines for my genetic mutation. But I began my research. I had Chris, I had my kids, my mother, my family, my friends, and my life. I soldiered on.

Dr. Stoopler had kept me alive several times so I could wait for the next superdrug. But this time, I was under siege knowing that time might not be on my side. Being unable to breathe causes a visceral response. I could practically smell my own fear.

A few weeks later, I had a stroke.

When I awoke, it slowly dawned on me that my right hand was numb. When I tried to get out of bed and put weight on my hand, I collapsed back on my side. Even though I could see my hand, I couldn't feel it.

I turned to tell Chris, but I could not speak. My tongue would not work; my mouth felt strange and awkward. I tried not to panic, but I was terrified.

This time, Chris took me back to Stamford Hospital, where I was admitted through the ER.

As we'd hurriedly packed my things, I reminded him to put my "lucky bag" in with my stuff. I kept it ready, under my desk, for all my trips to the hospital. I could not speak, but I pointed with my left hand so Chris would not forget it. My lucky bag was just a big, soft sack, and in it I kept the following:

- my wedding invitation;
- a tiny string doll made by my favorite nephew, Joshua, along with a picture of him;
- one "I love you" card from Chris;

- one picture of Rachel and me, dressed to kill, taken at a fancy party;
- one birthday card from Mom and Dad; and
- a picture of Michael and me holding hands, our backs to the camera, taken on a trip to Mount Herzl in Israel. We were going up the hill. There was an innocence to that photo that I loved. No one knew then the future that lay in store for us all.

That lucky bag had worked for a long time. I needed it to keep on working.

I had to tell Michael and Rachel that I'd had a stroke and was in the hospital again. I stole a phrase from one of the doctors, who told me the stroke was like "a bubble in my brain." I liked that imagery and found it useful in my quest to keep my children informed without worrying them too much.

"Just a little bubble in my brain," I told Rachel and Michael in separate phone conversations from my room in the hospital. "But I seem to be improving now. The feeling in my hand is returning, and I can speak and think much more clearly. To help my circulation, they have me sitting up on a chair that looks like a BarcaLounger, and I'm in an ultramodern, gigantic private room that feels a bit like a spaceship with all this modern equipment. And I do have a great view! How are you? What's going on?"

As usual in conversations like this one, Rachel asked for a few more details.

"Are you really getting the feeling back in your hand? Did the stroke affect your speech? Because you sound fine to me. Are Chris or Grandma in the room with you right now?" She wanted a fuller picture of me getting back to health, surrounded by loved ones, despite the worrisome truth that I was subjected to yet another trauma.

Michael listened, often pausing and halted in his responses to my detailed explanations. I wanted to tell him what he needed to know, but I could feel his discomfort and fear as he struggled with the best way to respond. I knew he just wanted to run for the hills whenever these calls from me arrived. When he was a little boy, he would shut his eyes tight and scream "No!" when I said it was time for bed, or he'd duck under the water when I said he had to get out of the pool—like the character in the movie *The Wiz*, who sang a show-stopping number called "Don't bring Me No Bad News." In this case, I surfed quickly from my own frightening update to his far more normal world with an abrupt change of topic. "How is the hunt for the new house coming along?"

Once again, I felt the thinness of the tightrope between giving them information and trying not to worry them. There must be a sensitivity when telling people about serious illness. I was not the only one who lived with cancer. It was my beloved husband, my children, my ex-wife, my family, and my friends. I always wanted to ease the blow, knowing that it was harder on them to live with my cancer than it was for me. They deserved to be treated this way.

As I figured out my options for the next treatment, I felt dread. I reminded myself that the hardest time was always between treatment plans. Once I started on the new path, I would feel better, just as I had in the past.

As long as I had my oxygen, I was mobile. That was all that mattered.

~

I had a triumvirate of supportive, brilliant oncologists, two in New York and one in Boston. I consulted with them all. I also reached out to my old teams at the pharmaceutical companies, Pfizer and Novartis, to see if there were any new drugs in the pipeline that my doctors were not yet aware of. In between, I refused to give in to my fears.

The activity calmed me. I knew the coping mechanisms that had worked for me in the past. I was good at fact-gathering. I needed to tell the people I loved that I was starting anew, against all the odds but with the best medical minds on my team. Once I got my emotions out and the facts straight, and the best options had been transformed into the next treatment, I would feel better. Then it would become a mission that I would carry out. With the support and love of my family, I moved into army general mode, ready for the next battle. I was fighting for myself and for them, too.

I refused to stop living. I kept working at the synagogue, going to New York to see the shows I loved, and cherishing evenings at home with Chris. When we curled up together on the couch, watching TV or a movie, I experienced a heightened sense of love, a deeper thrill to his caress as he massaged my feet or my back. I thought of a song I loved called "Fifty Percent" from the show *Ballroom* about a woman who loved a married man. She no longer cared that she could not have all of him. She took what she could get and appreciated it. Chris and I were compromised as well. We didn't know how long we had, but each moment we did have felt sweeter, and on that chenille sofa, we shut our minds to thoughts of new treatment plans and our uncertain future and just held onto the moment.

Rachel and I kept up our long tradition of attending Wednesday matinees on Broadway, since she was not teaching over the summer, and we even took a trip to the Canyon Ranch health spa in Massachusetts, when I had no choice but to cancel our planned trip to Berlin.

Our spa trip was a dream. I was able to let go and accept help because letting people help you is what spas are about. The staff transported my oxygen tanks everywhere for me, removing the empty cartridges and bringing me full ones. The hotel had no steps, so I was able to get around easily, and I felt grateful I could still spend this time with Rachel. We called it the YES hotel, because all they said was *yes*. Yes, you can have a room near the elevator. Yes, you can have a midday smoothie. Yes, we can send a housekeeper to turn down the beds early. Yes, we can arrange to take you around the Berkshires and to a nearby restaurant. Anything at all we could think we needed, we got. But mostly we stayed right there in the hotel, luxuriating in each other's company. We even took a spin class together, despite my reliance upon the oxygen. I was happy that she left me to get a mandatory massage. I knew she was straddling the line between believing I was getting better and wanting to make sure I didn't need her at every moment.

Rachel was confident that my doctors would come up with the next course of treatment. Despite my history of setbacks, I had repeatedly recovered, and Rachel had enough experience to understand the process. Whatever doubts she might have been having privately, her voice never gave her away.

Michael was more reticent, often finding it difficult to choose the words to discuss what he did not want to think about. I could feel his discomfort over the phone, and I did not challenge him. I just kept plugging on, dogged in my determination to keep the love flowing, even if he could not express his own emotions back to me.

I knew they were used to talking to their mother about me, letting out emotions with her that they hid from me. Once again, I thanked God for Jodi, who protected them when I could not.

Jodi's father, Lou, had died quickly and unexpectedly from pancreatic cancer while we were still married. She was forty-two at the time. His love for her and all his grandchildren was part of the background drumbeat of our lives. Jodi handled his death with sorrow and strength. I took heart from her example, knowing how impressionable Michael and Rachel were at that adolescent stage. They loved their grandfather as much as anyone in their lives. They saw Jodi and her mother remain steadfast even in the face of death. Somehow, even when he was taken from her, Jodi managed to keep the bounty of her father's love inside her. In her, my children had the perfect example of grief and recovery.

There were thirteen options for treatment, but none offered the comfort level I had felt in the past. There were no great new drugs in the pipeline for my genetic code. The newest drug, offered by Dr. Shaw, the eminent doctor in Boston, was so new it was extremely risky. I would be one of the first patients to try this drug. Chris wanted me to try the drug. He believed wholeheartedly in Dr. Shaw, who was brilliant, skillful, and emotive.

"She's young," he admitted. "But she's at the forefront of all the newest treatments in the field. She's already had startling successes in her ongoing drug trials. Yes, it's risky, but you need to do something radical."

I realized he was begging. Chris, who was not by nature a risk taker, was desperate.

Dr. Stoopler, my trusted doctor in New York who had saved my life so many times, disagreed. He wanted me to take a drug that offered the benefit of battling any potential brain cancer as well as lung cancer, and pair that drug with an old-line chemotherapy that was nonspecific for my genetic mutation. He thought this option offered me the best chance until a better drug became available.

I was wavering. Dr. Shaw's plan was radical. Dr. Stoopler's plan was conservative. I had been at such pivotal decision-making points before. I knew I had to think it through and make the best decision I could at that time and place. That much, I'd learned.

Chris and I had a pact we had forged early in our relationship. We were fifty-something when we met, adults with our own long histories. We agreed that at important decision-making junctures in our lives, we would listen to each other's point of view but ultimately allow the other to make his own decisions without guilt. If necessary, we would agree to disagree. And neither of us would say, "I told you so."

My mother and I conferred. Unlike Chris, who was relatively new to this game, she was a veteran in the battle. She, too, wanted to follow Dr. Stoopler's advice.

I sided with my mother against my lover, but she was my medical brain, my most fierce advocate, and I trusted her judgment implicitly.

I went with Dr. Stoopler's treatment plan. He had saved me so many times. I hoped he had one more trick up his sleeve. As I decided upon this conservative but intelligent choice, I knew I needed another miracle.

Life Goes On...Thankfully

~

I wanted no part of unfinished business, and that meant practical matters had to be addressed. Once a year, I updated my will. Of course, Michael and Rachel were my first concern, but this year, I had a new love in my life to consider. I had a husband. Luckily, Chris did not need my money. Chris, a man with no children of his own and a lifetime of work and conservative spending habits, was going to be just fine financially.

But what about Jodi? Jodi had made my gay life possible. I could never, never forget that. It was she who allowed my lovers to sit at the family holiday tables over the years. It was she who went back to work after our divorce was finalized. Her love for me was a constant that receded into the background but never faded.

"Jodi has to make a wedding for Rachel," I told Chris, knowing that I would be generous to her in my will and hoping he could see that I wanted the three of them to be able to live as if I were still there, that I could not abandon my responsibilities to them, even in death.

I thought of a song from the show *Dear Evan Hansen*. The song is called "So Big/So Small." A little boy who loved trucks was overjoyed to find a big truck in his driveway one morning. At first, he didn't comprehend that the truck was there because his father was moving out of the house. But that night, he asked his mother if there would be another truck the next day to take his mother away, too. No, she swore; she'd be there, no matter what.

I couldn't say that to my kids. I couldn't promise that I'd be there no matter what. Jodi was the one who was there for them, no matter what.

~

"Richard, do you already have the rugulah for your shiva in your freezer?" My friends knew me well. My obsessiveness with planning was a running joke.

"I refuse to be buried under the Van Wyck Expressway," I always said, as my friends and I headed from Manhattan through Queens to Long Island on many a car trip. We would all stare in a kind of muted horror at the cemeteries within view of the highway, the thousands upon thousands of gray soot-covered stones, many of which had a Jewish star on the top or face. Apparently, these are an historic and interesting cluster of burial grounds, replete with famous names like composers Martin Hamlisch and Lorenz Hart. But even though my parents had a family plot in one of those Jewish cemeteries, where I was most welcome, I had a different vision.

Unlike most synagogues, my synagogue in Connecticut had a beautiful cemetery adjacent to the temple, set amid luxurious, velvety-green grounds. I had broken with tradition many times, and I created a new one yet again with my burial arrangements. I arranged for a plot at Beth El Cemetery in Stamford.

After the funeral service in our beautiful Stamford synagogue, my casket could be placed on a roller and simply wheeled by the pallbearers out to the gravesite. No need for the mourners to get in the car and drive for an hour and then submit to the long lines and confusion about where to go to find my grave. Everyone would love me for this, I knew. I thought of it as kind of a final gift.

I created instructions for my funeral service. Who should speak? Of course, my brothers. My very closest friends, my rabbi and cantor from Wyckoff, and my rabbi from Stamford. Jodi and my children at the end. And, throughout it all, the pièce de résistance, the synagogue's cantor, who would, I knew, blend prayer with my favorite Broadway songs. The effect would be so hauntingly beautiful that everyone would feel they had been to a Great Funeral.

I was hell-bent on creating efficient email lists for the shiva notice. I wanted Chris, Jodi, my mother, and my kids to know that all they had to do was press SEND, and everyone would be notified. I knew they might have computer issues, especially if they were grieving and stressed. I actually had three lists. Family, friends, and medical people. I wanted the information about my demise to be disseminated quickly and easily. I certainly did not want a paltry turnout. I wanted a packed house.

I also included one last instructive email to the custodial staff of the synagogue—I wanted to make sure they had extra chairs ready. Oh and yes, I also left instructions for a table upon which to place the very best photos of my life, and a second table near the exit for goody bags and water bottles.

After all, a lot of them would have a long drive home.

Epilogue

Rabbis and Rugulah

"Do Not Stand At My Grave And Weep"

I am not there: I do not sleep.
I am a thousand winds that blow,
I am the diamond glints on the snow,
I am the sun on ripened grain,
I am the gentle autumn rain.
When you awaken in the morning's hush
I am the swift uplifting rush
Of quiet birds in circled flight.
I am the soft stars that shine at night.
Do not stand at my grave and cry,
I am not there; I did not die.

~Mary Elizabeth Frye

I learned of Richard's death the day after Rosh Hashanah, the Jewish New Year. A few weeks earlier, he'd sent me a lovely New Year's card. It was still perched on my kitchen windowsill and read: "Sending wishes for good health, happiness, and a bit of sweetness throughout the coming year! Lots of love, Richard and Chris."

No one sent more cards than Richard did. New Year's cards were an annual tradition, but birthday cards were his bread and butter. He sent out more than three hundred a year to friends and family. He often sent special "thinking of you" messages as well. Chris once showed me a bawdy one he had gotten from Richard, when reminiscing with me about Richard's irreverent sense of humor. There was a picture of Richard in the nude, with a big smile on his face, and a big Japanese paper fan covering his penis. It read, "I love you THIS much."

Chris was the one who called me in the early evening with the news of Richard's death. As soon as I saw Chris's name on my caller ID, I knew Richard was gone. In a wave of visceral denial, I stuck with the usual pleasantries in a vain attempt to forestall the inevitable.

"Hi, Chris. Happy New Year. How are you?"

"Okay, and you?" His voice was clear, the timbre strong and melodious.

"I'm fine."

I wasn't fine. I felt an eerie disconnect from what was sure to follow, and my stomach muscles tightened up as if I were preparing to catch a heavy ball.

I sat at the edge of my bed. I let just a few extra seconds pass, and then invited him to tell me the disastrous news. "What's going on?"

"Well, I'm not really okay. Richard passed away yesterday."

I felt a swift, immediate recoil, as if I could shove the words and the truth away, and a simultaneous, gut-wrenching feeling of despair. Richard always said his life was possible because of biology, chemistry, timing, and good luck. His luck, so astonishing for so long, had run out. He was only fifty-seven.

Like so many others, I loved and admired Richard. He wanted to write a book about his life, and I have been privileged to help him. Our weekly sessions had become a part of my life. His bravery often astonished me, both when he left a comfortable, enviable family life in the suburbs to reconstruct a whole new one as a gay man, and in his valiant fight against a deadly disease. His passions—love, loyalty, generosity, and philanthropy, always paired with a wicked sense of humor—were legendary to all who knew him.

I really thought he was invincible, even as I watched with a mix of awe and discomfort as he dragged those oxygen tanks around in the last few months. Only two weeks earlier, he'd visited me in Westport to attend a special production of *Falsettos* at the Westport Country Playhouse. I was so happy I had something to offer him that I knew he would like.

I was glad he came, but it made me nervous to see him out in public. I usually saw him at his apartment in Stamford, where he was in a contained space with no steps, and things felt much safer. Once out in the world, he seemed terribly fragile. I worried about the three small steps he had to climb to find his seat in the theater.

I had visited him in the hospital two months before his death, when he was on the precipice of his decline. Even there, sitting in his big hospital Barcalounger, he seemed as if he was still in control. He was beating back his illness with his customary charm, optimism, and a keen grasp of the medical facts. He was employing his winning ways with the staff, whose good favor he cultivated with ease. Even then, though, I could see that Richard's luck was running out. Something about the endless parade of medical staff all asking the same questions made me believe there were no more answers for Richard.

Chris told me that Richard's oxygen level had fallen so low he could scarcely breathe, even with the supplemental oxygen. They took one last emergency ride to the hospital, where Richard was admitted to Intensive Care, but it was clear that his one battered lung was failing. He was placed on a ventilator. He could not speak. Jodi and Rachel came immediately to the hospital to see him and hold his hands. A cell phone was propped up to his ear so he could hear Michael say one last good-bye from his home in California.

"Dad," they all heard Michael say, "I love you. I always have, and I always will. You are the best dad in the world."

Richard became agitated and had to be sedated and then finally fell sleep. Chris insisted that no medical personnel wake him up for any reason—he could not bear the thought that Richard would be disturbed. He told me that he had fallen asleep in the

Life Goes On...Thankfully

chair next to Richard's bed and was awakened suddenly when Richard, muted by the ventilator, threw a pillow at him. He wrote Chris a note.

I'm afraid. Please lay down next to me.

Chris got in the bed and held Richard tight, crying, while Richard grew quiet. Very soon after, Richard's heart stopped beating. His David and Goliath battle with lung cancer had come to an end.

The funeral was held at the same synagogue in which Richard and Chris had been such active members. It was a beautiful synagogue, set back in the most serene, countrified part of Stamford, Connecticut. The sanctuary was very large, with circular, inclusive seating that easily accommodated the very large crowd that appeared that day. There were hundreds of people in attendance, every one of us certain that we were one of Richard's best friends.

He had always told me he was no good at acting. Perhaps not, but I believe none of us thought he would really die. His skill as a writer, producer, and director was evident that day. All of his funeral instructions were found on his computer in a file marked, Upon My Death.

The funeral was spellbinding. Richard had chosen the prayers, the musical selections, and all the speakers. He allotted everyone a specific amount of time to speak (three minutes or less).

There were eloquent eulogies by rabbis from New Jersey and Connecticut and a cantor whose voice rivaled Broadway's best. Her mournful tone and plaintive rendering of the Hebrew prayers released a collective sadness and reduced us all to tears.

Richard's three brothers, whom I could never keep straight, Ronnie, Randy, and Robert, spoke first. They were big men with trembling voices. Robert referred to his brother as "One Singular Sensation," borrowing the words from the title of the hit song in the Broadway classic, *A Chorus Line*.

His college roommate and lifelong friend, David, recounted their early days at Northwestern University, where they met. In those days, you were defined by your music preferences. David said he should have known then that Richard was gay from the Barbra Streisand and Julie Andrews LPs.

His dear friend Marcy recalled a song they both loved called "Old Friend," from the show *Getting My Act Together and Taking It on the Road*. The song highlights the disappointments of a life filled with a parade of lovers who fall away, and the unwavering desire to keep searching till it's right, no matter what the cost. I recalled the fervent search for love that Richard described to me in the years after he came out, the single-mindedness with which he pursued finding the all-important love of his life, and his great joy when he realized he had. But even as he found his great love, Chris, he was well aware of the risks inherent in their blissful union.

Richard told me this story. "Chris and I were sitting together on the sofa in the living room, where we sat after dinner, snuggling and watching TV. Chris wasn't feeling well, and he was wrapped in a blanket that Jodi had given him for Hanukkah. I saw his fragility at that moment. I wondered for the umpteenth time if it was wrong of me to let him fall in love with me. Surely, I had a responsibility to say to him, "I'm gonna die before you do. Is this an investment you really want to make? I might not even make it past the apartment lease…But I didn't say any of that. I loved him too much."

Then Richard recalled several lines from the show *Falsettos*. In the second act, after the main character has finally, painfully come out of the closet to his wife and son, and his lover, Whizzer, is dying of AIDS, the question is asked, "Would you make the same decisions again?" And the answer is, "I'd like to believe that I'd do it again and again."

"That's what I'd like Chris to say," Richard said, with tears in his eyes.

Jodi was among the last to speak, an honor bestowed upon her by her ex-husband. The journey she had taken with Richard was fraught with love and loss and ultimately, acceptance. I admired her all over again, a woman who had taken a path she never expected or planned for, and then created her own workable adaptation. She was not frozen in time. She was not bitter. She had been able to adapt to her new reality and live a new life, one she had not chosen but that she ultimately embraced. I watched her rise and walk to the bimah, knowing every eye was upon her. I watched her capture the audience with her direct, straightforward words. She had more than fulfilled her responsibility as a wife, the loving mother of their two children, and the woman willing, no matter how difficult the task, to fashion a role for herself and her children in the revised playbook in which they all found themselves.

"Richard was the most authentic person I ever knew," she said to us and to her children. "And we are truly a modern family."

Even as she credited Richard, I credited her, remembering his oft-stated gratitude that it was she who made possible his life as a gay man with strong and enduring connections to his children.

Rachel, a Daddy's girl if ever there was one, stood willowy and graceful at the bimah, buttressed by her brother and mother. She was composed and radiant despite her evident sorrow, a young woman of twenty-six. We all ached for her loss, the father who had been the envy of all her friends, who dreaded that he might not be able to walk her down the aisle at her wedding, who would not see her babies if she had them, who would no longer be there to take her on trips to the farthest reaches of the world or sit at a holiday table for a family dinner.

She recalled the monthly Broadway shows that were their tradition, her voice breaking. I knew she wondered how she would go on without him. But she had her father's strength as well as his love. The last words of her eulogy were, "Life goes on, thankfully."

Michael, twenty-eight, rose to the occasion and spoke eloquently as he recalled the Jets games; the trips to Israel, Switzerland, and faraway beaches; and the shared nights in Manhattan apartments, where Richard allowed Michael and his friends to indulge in TV and beer.

Richard's mother, Audrey, bowed and tiny, such a great force in his life, did not speak.

His husband, Chris, tall and so attractive, even in grief, did not speak.

When it was all over, six pallbearers carefully rolled Richard's casket out of the synagogue to the peaceful adjacent cemetery, where the freshly dug plot awaited.

The sun was shining, and the prayers were traditional. We all said Kaddish: the mourner's prayer. Someone held a black umbrella over the head of Richard's mother, so she would not suffer in the afternoon sun as mourners, one by one, came forward to put a shovelful of dirt into the grave.

Richard had given us all one last gift. The cemetery was as serene as he had hoped, lush and green, with dappled light on that warm day. Even as we stepped away from the gravesite, no one really wanted to leave Richard there alone. But we all eventually filed back into the synagogue for the sustenance we knew would follow. Rabbis and rugulah, the Jewish tradition. There was a table loaded with hundreds of photos of Richard's life, with pictures of everyone present. I caught myself crying when I came upon a picture of my own daughter and Rachel at their nursery-school graduation more than two decades earlier.

Finally, at a long table near the exit, there were small, colorful goody bags filled with Raisinets and water bottles for the long ride home. Richard had thought of everything.

—Bonnie Adler

About the Author

Bonnie Adler of Westport, Connecticut, and Palm Beach Gardens, Florida, is a writer and reporter. This is her first book.

Made in United States
North Haven, CT
03 February 2022

15594845R00150